PATHWAYS TO ANARCHISM

For Amelia with love

Pathways to Anarchism

PHILIP EDWARDS
Senior Lecturer in Philosophy,
Education Faculty, Monash University

Ashgate

Aldershot • Brookfield USA • Singapore • Sydney

Published by
Ashgate Publishing Limited
Gower House
Croft Road
Aldershot
Hants GU11 3HR
England

Ashgate Publishing Company
Old Post Road
Brookfield
Vermont 05036
USA

British Library Cataloguing in Publication Data
Edwards, Philip, 1923-
  Pathways to anarchism
  1.Anarchism 2.State, The 3.Individualism
  I.Title.
  320.5'7

Library of Congress Catalog Card Number: 97-71461

ISBN 1 85972 639 9

Printed in Great Britain by Antony Rowe Ltd, Chippenham, Wiltshire

Contents

Acknowledgements

This essay had its beginnings as a PhD thesis, written under the supervision of Dr Len O'Neill of the Department of Philosophy at Melbourne University. Such merit as the argument has is due in very large part to the searching, critical and kindly guidance he provided and for that I am very grateful to him. My thanks to him also for the title of the book.

During 1986-7 I was a Visiting Scholar with the Social and Political Sciences Committee at Cambridge University. My early researches on the topic benefitted greatly from access to its resources and post-graduate seminars. In particular I thank Professor John Dunn firstly for securing the billet for me. Secondly, for the benefit of several conversations I had with him on the topic which helped greatly in steadying the course of my wayward intellectual imagination.

I wish to thank Neil and Frances Courtney for allowing so many dinner table and other conversations to be dominated by the topic of anarchism and my voice on the subject. One could not hope for a more forbearing audience or more gentle critics.

My greatest debt is to Amelia whose confidence in this protracted project and friendship never faltered, even on the darkest days. The book has also benefitted from her lightning intelligence, her ability to cut to the centre of an issue, putting aside the distractions around it.

What infelicities remain do so on account of my wilful refusal to attend more carefully to the arguments and advice of these five people.

Preface

Working from the perspective of possessive individualism (without implying that I accept that to be the full compass of human nature), this book challenges the widely held liberal belief that possessive individualists need states to restrain them from trespassing on the natural rights of others and harming themselves.

In chapter 1 I show how Hobbes argues, in his answer to the Foole, that it is rational to co-operate voluntarily in a state of nature and consistent with natural rights to prefer (under certain conditions) the state of nature to the commonwealth.

But can anarchy be sufficiently sustained to accommodate the long-term self-interests of possessive individualists? In chapter 2 the question is tested against one form of libertarian anarchism which, however, is found to be vulnerable to decay into self-defeating (or entropic) anarchy.

So, in chapter 3 another libertarian approach to anarchy is sampled which implies that anarchy will always degenerate and that a minimal state will have to be created to protect natural rights holders. However, I argue against that view; given a certain social structure, natural rights can be protected in a state of nature. It follows that anarchy will not always degenerate into self-defeating anarchy. In the general field of possessive individualism Hobbes proves to be more far-sighted than those theorists who insist that *only* the state or *only* anarchy is both viable and legitimate. He saw a case for both.

The rest of the book, from chapter 5 onwards, expands on an idea used as a counter-example to the inevitability of (at least) a minimal state. The expansion exercise is intended to show how an anarchic community can be designed to protect itself from degeneration into entropic anarchy and the need for a state. Firstly, the putatively utopian idea of unanimous direct democracy is modified slightly, in chapter 5, to show how, in practical terms, when members of the community obey its laws they are obeying their own wills. That reduces the distance between rulers and ruled to vanishing point.

But the practical solution is short of the utopian ideal. The community still has to reckon on the presence of free riders and requires means to preserve itself from the damage they bring about. This is managed, in chapter 6, through a socio-legal system which, in the first place, makes free riding itself a costly and unattractive proposition. Secondly, when it occurs, in spite of being so risky, the acephalous community has very efficient means to rid itself of transgressors.

The final matter discussed, in chapter 7, is tactics to avoid large wealth differentials creating internal conflicts in the community without having to use centralised coercive methods to redistribute wealth. Two approaches are discussed. The former is rejected in favour of the latter on the grounds of empirical feasibility.

Anarchism, I conclude, is a viable option for possessive individualists which, moreover, does not require them to compromise their natural rights as the state, even a minimal state, will. Though modern liberal democratic states are sometimes held up as paradigm custodians of natural rights, and therefore legitimated on that ground, yet they are by no means the only legitimate form of polity (on those terms).

1 The political options for possessive individualists

In modern history, one of the best known putative political deducements that sovereign states are Hobson's Choice is Hobbes'.[1] A considerable amount of modern commentary reveals fastidious disinclination to find merit with his argument that subjects (subjects, not citizens) must surrender their natural rights to an absolute sovereign in order to preserve peace. Yet there is something equivocal about regard for Hobbes. Michael Taylor, in his *Community, Anarchy & Liberty* (1982, chapter 6) makes the point that, in fact, liberal justifications for states owe a great deal to Hobbesian - and Humean - thought; that the shape and boundaries of modern statist justifications were articulated towards the beginning of the modern era by Hobbes and Hume. It is widely believed the limits of Hobbes' political possibilities are set by the presumed fact that anarchy is always self-defeating so the theoretical options are binary exclusive:

1   Either anarchy or archy,
2   Anarchy is always self-defeating.
_____
3   Therefore archy (of a kind which countervails anarchic tendencies).

In recent years this approach to understanding Hobbes has been carefully developed and refined by George Kavka, the full extent and summary of whose argument is in his *Hobbesian Moral & Political Theory* (1986). There he explains that it is in the logic of the structure of the state of nature that the incidence of violence can only escalate and intensify. Where two or more agents are gathered together in the state of nature and they covet the same goods (even domination of one over the others), they are dispositionally condemned to a spiral of pre-emptive attacks - I shall return to this, below. The only alternative is sovereign government capable of the means needed to restrain would-be combatants.

In this chapter I will join company with Kavka and others in their reading of Hobbes' account of human dispositions. In particular, a refinement of this - Macpherson's (1962) characterisation of it as possessive individualism - will be especially useful. Possessive individualism will be used generically, throughout to stand for both a dispositional and argumentative perspective. Presently it will serve the effort to show that there is more than one political option open even when the mean dispositional stock is assumed to be fixed and uniform; it helps to indicate that there is more to political philosophy than (merely) working out the respective rights and duties of government and governed. Part of the undertaking, and a focus for attention in this chapter, will be to show that possessive individualism (PI'sm) does not form the major premiss in a compelling argument for the necessity of states. Here I part company from those who read Hobbes as unequivocally statist. Using Hobbes' own terms, it will be disputed here that PI'sm in the state of nature makes the state of nature one of self-defeating anarchy. Contrary to widely received opinion, Hobbes actually anticipated the necessary condition required for anarchy to be practicable. He had an insight into political possibilities (e.g. for acephalous society) which have been neglected or overlooked in the main body of modern political thought. Of course this does not mean that Hobbes was really an anarchist, albeit cleverly disguised.[2] It simply means he anticipated what anarchists since have claimed, viz. life without sovereign states is not necessarily self-defeating. In that sense it is possible to regard some of his argument as proto-anarchic. But there is another side to Hobbes' proto-anarchism. On the one hand he points to the necessary condition for acephalous society but, on the other, he does not attend to the sufficient conditions. This bias gives the argument for the state some fiat. And Hobbes' moves are, revealingly, replicated in recent arguments, even ones which do not appear to owe him much. But that is to pre-empt chapter 2.

2

To defer discussion no further and, since it is a concept which is going to be put to considerable use, we begin with possessive individualism. Agents, it is believed, are beings who possess natural rights, and for these rights, nothing is owed to any other agent. The primary natural right of any political consequence is an entitlement to liberty of action free from coercion.[3] PIs have no intuitive deontological regard for other individuals. This is partly the reason for an incipient problem with them, namely their predisposition to renege on agreements. However, mindful that, in the long term, this can result in more harm than good, they often accept some measure of preventative control. Some PIs accept government as an enabling device to ensure orderly exchanges amongst them through the centralisation of public security. Generally speaking, apart from providing, and probably exacting payment for, public security, government agents are regarded by PIs as having no legitimate powers to interfere in their lives and doings. Public security activity is warranted only when an agent's actions invade the natural and derivative rights of others. One such derivative right is to material property which is had by accessing nature, laying claim to it and, perhaps, working it - mixing labour with it, as Locke said. Property may be exchanged, bequeathed or otherwise given away. Its owners have the right to exclude others from it though, we should add, it can be forfeited in a jural society, e.g. if its holder has trespassed on another's rights and is obliged to compensate. There are differences amongst PIs, of course, for instance they tolerate varying degrees of social control and disagree about the legitimate limits to which property can be alienated,[4] but it is tantamount to a self-contradiction for them to deny the belief that their natural rights have moral precedence.

Hobbes worked with this basic material, albeit property rights play a subsidiary role in his thought. His undertaking was to work out the costs in natural rights to buy peace. As I have foreshadowed, he was rather less didactic on this point than is often thought. To this issue we now turn.

Hobbes' writings, *Leviathan* in particular, received considerable attention, though not always acclaim, particularly during the Restoration period from 1660. Amongst his severest critics then were Bishop Bramhall and Lord Clarendon. It is received opinion[5] that, for all their stridency, these critics were light in philosophical acumen, depending instead on dogma and rhetoric with which to attack Hobbes.

Yet it is to Bramhall and Clarendon that we must give due for being amongst the first to detect the proto-anarchic threads in Hobbes' political thought. They probably went too far in suspecting Hobbes was an anarchic fifth columnist within the King's Court; nevertheless we can follow their leads to the point where Bramhall picks out what I shall call Hobbes' escape clause and Clarendon suspects the social contract is politically redundant. From these points I shall try to indicate how Hobbes was not just a statist or really a crypto-anarchist but, rather, a man who detected the political possibilities and limitations of both. True, he is relatively circumspect in his handling of anarchic possibilities and who would not be in his position ... writing such material was treason and treason was a capital offence. In recognising both as possibilities, Hobbes, so early in the development of modern political theory, had an uncommon grasp of the political features which lay the foundations of much of the argument to follow.

So as to be quite clear about what I am doing, an outline of Hobbesian human dispositions and the other circumstances of political life are now needed. He says that humans have involuntary and voluntary motions, appetites for those things which enhance motions and aversions to those which impede them. Humans also have faculties: memory (of experiences), prudence (the ability to learn from experiences) and reason (ratiocination). The faculties help humans to deliberate on and intervene in events so as to enhance motions. For any process of deliberation, the final endeavour - towards or away from something - is called an act of will. Desires are characteristically self-interested (PI) and the politically most significant are those for self-preservation and "a perpetuall and restless desire for Power after power, that ceaseth only in death" (1968, p.161). Success in self-preservation is a measure of able use of the faculties. These are the essential features of Hobbes' psychology.

The essential political circumstances are: (1) that humans have liberty-rights (or natural rights, they come to the same thing, though it is important to remember they are pre-legal) and (2) there is, universally, a law of nature. Natural right is:

> ... the Liberty each man hath, to use his own power, as he will himselfe, for the preservation of his own Nature; that is to say, his own Life, ... of doing anything ... he shall conceive to be the aptest means thereunto. (1968, p.189)

4

Natural law is:

> ... a Precept, or generall Rule, found out by Reason, by which a man
> is forbidden to do, that, which is destructive of his life ... (p.189)

Hobbes distinguishes rational from irrational appetites. For
instance, a person might initiate war now to achieve some short-term
goal though this action risks the agent's violent and untimely death.
This is irrational because the action jeopardises the primary desire for
life free from hurt and untimely death. It is rational to proceed in a
manner conducive to the primary desire. Fortunately, the faculty of
reason detects "convenient Articles of Peace" - the laws of nature -
which, in as much as they serve the primary appetite, it is rational to
comply with.

Individuals, even though they perceive the sense of the laws of
nature, can only count on their personal resources to gain them their
ends. Personal resources, such as wit and strength, are unevenly
distributed amongst people but there is an averaging effect: strength
can be outwitted, wit can be crushed by strength, those two combined in
one might be defeated by a confederation, confederates can be outwitted
etc. And:

> ... if any two men desire the the same thing, which neverthelesse
> they cannot both enjoy, they become enemies; and in this way to
> their End, (which is principally their owne conservation, and
> sometimes their delectation only,) endeavour to destroy, or subdue
> one another ... if one plant, sow, build, or possesse a convenient
> Seat, other may probably be expected to come prepared with forces
> united, to dispossesse, and deprive him, not only of the fruit of his
> labour, but also of his life, or liberty. And the Invader is in like
> danger of another. (p.184)

Self-defeating anarchy? Dispositions and circumstances combined
give very much that appearance. Particularly since violence does not run
in plain cycle. This has been alluded to above, but to expand slightly: if
an agent, A, appropriates some good, x, she creates a scarcity for
everybody else with regard to x. If A is not a fool she will realise that her
appropriation makes her liable to attack from any and all who want x
too. Suppose she has grounds for expecting an attack. The stakes are, in

5

fact, higher than just x; they include her liberty, even her life. A's chances of surviving, as the possessor of x preferably, are increased if she takes the initiative with a pre-emptive (and surprise) strike at her would-be attackers. However, her opposition will also realise this is her best move (so long as they are not fools); it follows that its best move is to pre-empt A's first move. There is no theoretical upper limit to the moves in this game once it has begun. If we assume, realistically enough, that individuals will not be involved with just one but several "warres", as Hobbes calls them, at a time, it is no great strain on the imagination to see that the spiralling effect increases everybody's chances of losing. Whereas this state of nature was an experimental fiction by Hobbes, part of his transposition of Galileo's hypothetical methodology to the social sciences, nonetheless something remarkably akin to it is an endemic fear in our ordinary lives:

> Let [a sceptic] therefore consider with himselfe, when taking a journey, he armes himselfe, and seeks to go well accompanied; when going to sleep, he locks his dores; even when in his house he locks his chests ... Does he not there as much accuse mankind by his actions, as I do by my words? (pp.186-7)

The question now is: is this degenerative process, as Nozick will come to call it, of the state of nature irreversibly on course with self-defeating anarchy? Is there nothing to be done, except contract one's way out of the state of nature?

Of the thirty-odd laws of nature enumerated by Hobbes, it is from amongst the first three we begin to find our answer. The first law of nature is to endeavour peace in as much as there is hope of obtaining it; otherwise people have recourse to "warre" (p.190). The second law prescribes that people be willing to lay down their natural rights, in the endeavour of peace, to the same extent that others are so willing. The third dictates that people abide by their contracts (p.201). With these propositions in hand, Hobbes sketches a four[6] step case for inventing the state:

1   self preservation is a natural imperative,
2   but the state of nature jeopardises self preservation,

3 however, reason discovers the laws of nature which, if implemented, countervail the state of nature,

4 therefore implement the laws of nature.

But, steps 1-4 do not, by themselves, give any assurance for a contented life; they are, by themselves:

> ... without the terrour of some Power, to cause them to be observed, ... contrary to our naturall Passions, that carry us to Partiality, Pride, Revenge, and the like. And Covenants, without the Sword, are but Words, and of no strength to secure men at all. (p.120)

To overcome the problem the laws of nature must be secured in a robustly practical way it seems.

Hobbes' most apparent practical solution begins with the social contract. In the interests of brevity it is assumed that readers are familiar with the essentials of this. Suffice the simple reminder: in order to avoid the vicious spiral of violence in the state of nature, it is reasoned that people must institute a power over themselves which has sufficient resources to coerce obedience to the laws of nature if need be. The act of institution is encapsulated in each and all individuals saying to the others:

> I AUTHORISE AND GIVE UP MY RIGHT TO GOVERNING MY SELFE, TO THIS Man ... on this condition, that thou give up thy Right to him [too]. (p.227)

In some passages Hobbes reads very uncompromisingly as to the purport here. The sovereign, that to which/whom the right of government is given up, expects from those who have authorised it/him "simple Obedience in all things" (p.395). And this extends to successive generations:

> But the People, for them and their Heirs, by the consent and Oaths, have long ago put the Supream Power of the Nation into the hands of their kings, for them and their Heirs ... (Hobbes, 1969, p.152)

Simple obedience in all things to a supreme power is arguably an incredible expectation for all but the most slavishly disposed, and certainly preposterous for Hobbesians who, as individuals, naturally love power for themselves and over others. Hobbes was aware of this protest and had an answer:

> If the soveraign command a man (...) to kill, wound, or mayme himselfe; or not to resist those that assault him; or to abstain from the use of food, ayre, medicine, or any other thing, without which he cannot live; yet hath that man the Liberty to disobey. (1968, pp.268-9)

And, if agents are subjected to any such commands the relationship between them and the sovereign regresses from civil society to that of the state of nature (see the second clause of the first law of nature, above). But the state of nature, apparently, is utterly self-defeating of any enterprise ... except suicide. Subjects who - rightly or wrongly - are commanded, as above, by the sovereign have no move open with the least chance of preserving their natures. Unless there is something in what I have advertised as Hobbes' escape clause and the political possibilities (as opposed to self-defeating qualities) of the state of nature.

We can begin with the escape clause; if escape from the commonwealth is needed and feasible, then it will be time to see if the state of nature is at least tolerable. The clue to the escape clause, detected early on by Bramhall, is followed up in the recent literature by Bowle (1969) and Hampton (1986). Bramhall objected to the retention of the right of nature in civil society on the grounds that it was permissive and a sham; it betrayed the fundamental duplicity in Hobbes' overt protestations in favour of absolute monarchy. In addition and, politically more essential, it (a) gave licence to resist arrest and other punitive measures and (b) left it to the discretion of subjects to decide if sovereign actions were threatening them to the point where they should invoke the second clause of the first law of nature. (a) and (b) both weaken the structural absoluteness of sovereignty. The commonwealth now appears to have government conditional on the "subjects'" satisfaction that it is not threatening them, and this is a matter open to continuous review by subjects. It follows that any perceived attempt at disagreeable enforcement by the government, far from being legitimate, is an act of war!

At a glance it might be objected to this reading of Hobbes that it is altogether too crude. In the first place government enforcement measures are nothing like so open to contention. Subjects and sovereign alike know that the state of nature is the worse alternative. Subjects will accommodate the wishes of government to any lengths so long as they reckon this will have less bad results than the state of nature. Resisting the sovereign, if it comes to that, is not a thing people choose to do; rather, it is a situation forced upon them. A corollary to this is the stark and vulnerable isolation of being at "warre" with the commonwealth. Nobody who has not been forced into it by the government will risk it and this tacitly implies no subjects not forced into war will risk their protection by succouring someone who is at war. Secondly, each act of war, of enforcement, by the government is directed at particulars; not only need it be of no concern to other subjects (other things being equal), it might actually be to their advantage:

> And this is the foundation of that right of Punishing, which is exercised in every Common-wealth. For the subjects did not give the Soveraign that right; but only in laying down theirs strengthened him to use his own, as he should think fit, for the preservation of them all. (Hobbes, 1968, p.354)

So, by attacking this or that subject, so far from weakening it, the act might, in fact, strengthen the government - by consolidating the support given it by non-threatened subjects.[7] In effect, appeal to the right of nature from within and against the commonwealth is a futile gesture, for who can long survive, unaided, a fight against the state? Bramhall might have lit upon a formal point but politically it is a man of straw. Locke, it might even be added, was surely the more perspicuous critic when he said of Hobbes' political system that it solved our problems with polecats by threatening us with lions.

But Hobbes was canny in his handling of lions and Bramhall did have an inkling of what he was about (and thoroughly disapproved of, too). Hobbes wrote:

> No man is bound ..., either to kill himselfe, or any other man; And consequently, ... the Obligation a man may sometimes have, upon the Command of the Soveraign to execute any dangerous, or

dishonourable Office, dependeth not on the Words of our Submission; but on the Intention; which is to be understood by the end thereof ... (p.269)

In other words subjects actually should obey the sovereign only if there is advantage in it for them. To be sure, there is no reason to suppose Hobbes wanted the state to be so fragile, so dependent on finicky consent, that it tottered on the brink of self-defeating anarchy. On the contrary, he had a trenchant loathing for political instability. At the same time, we have evidence here that he was not prepared to trade obedience at any price. Besides, it was not obedience which was of most importance to him (though it was to Bramhall); what was more important was what is exchanged for it:

The Obligation of Subjects to the Soveraign, is understood to last as long as, and no longer, than the power lasteth, by which he is able to protect them ... The end of Obedience is Protection. (p.272)

Bramhall was right, Hobbes had no particular affection for states in themselves. He was quite certain they are owed conditional obedience alone, viz. conditional on their providing protection of the peace.

But what if the state does not do this? Subjects can, and should, invoke the escape clause. Yet, is the result going to be an improvement? Mostly Hobbes seems to say that even bad states preserve more of civil society - the peace - than the state of nature possibly could. As witness to the Civil War, he had reason to write in this vein. But he did also write the escape clause and, as I have said, was taking a big enough risk in so doing. It is, therefore, testament to his courage and intellectual honesty that, in fact, he went further where the logic of his argument indicated an opening. The opening leads to the possibility of co-operative behaviour in the state of nature - and this from a man notorious in the history of ideas as being a champion of absolute government.

Hampton notes that Clarendon drew attention to the fact that, in *Leviathan*, the chapter introducing the laws of nature (chapter 14) follows immediately the chapter concerning the state of nature. Whatever the source of the laws of nature (commands of God, perhaps, but this is immaterial), they are declared by Hobbes to be "Immutable and Eternall". Moreover we have cognate access to them prior to entertaining the need for the commonwealth (the sovereign state). Not only are they cognised but seem to be feasible,

> ... in that [the laws of nature] require nothing but endeavour; he that endeavoureth their performance, fulfileth them. (p.215)

But if so, why resort to "warre" at all? In Clarendon's words:

> How should it else come to pass, that Mr. Hobbes, whilst he is demolishing the whole frame of Nature for want of order to support it, and makes it unavoidably necessary for every man to cut his neighbors throat ... I say, how comes it to pass, that ... he would in the same, and the next Chapter, set down such a Body of Laws prescribed by Nature itself, as are IMMUTABLE AND ETERNAL that there appears by his own shewing, a full remedy against all that confusion, for the avoiding whereof he hath devis'd all that unnatural and impossible Contract and Covenant? (Hampton, 1987, p.63)

It is, of course, the idea of a contract amongst the people to legitimise the office of sovereign to which Clarendon is objecting. But in doing that he stumbles on something else much more important for the present purpose. Admittedly he gets it slightly wrong. In the quotation from him, immediately above, he misidentifies the laws of nature as empirically determining whereas they are rational optimisers in Hobbes. But, like Bramhall, he nosed-out an argumentative depth in Hobbes far beyond the reach of a superficial reading of him. If we turn to Hobbes' famous answer to the "Foole" we realise that the laws of nature and certain consequences of them, though they do not render the social contract absurd, yet they make it theoretically redundant. We shall see how.

In the reply to the Foole, Hobbes (1968, pp.203-4) accounts for keeping our promises even in the state of nature for all that, elsewhere, he has spoken of promises as idle words without the sword to enforce them. I shall now try to show that the answer to the Foole provides the basis from which Hobbes could construct a socially possible state of nature which, evidently, cuts from under it the claim on behalf of the state that it must be created (and this, in turn, will advise our answer to

11

Nozick's minimal state in chapter 3). So, to the Foole: the third law of nature prescribes the performance of covenants made. The Foole counters: since he recognises no considerations save his own preservation and well-being, he complies with or breaks covenants as and when it suits him (p.203). Hobbes replies, this is faulty reasoning, even in the state of nature. "Where one of the parties has performed already," he says, it is reasonable for the second party to abide by the contract:

> ... in a condition of Warre, wherein every man to every man, ... is an Enemy, there is no man can hope by his own strength, or wit, to defend himselfe from destruction, without the help of Confederates; where every one expects the same defence by the Confederation, that any one else does: and therefore he which declares he thinks it reason to deceive those that help him, can in reason expect no other means of safety than what can be had from his owne Power. (pp.204-5)

If it is rational for the second party to perform its side of an agreement it is likewise for the first. If so, then the same goes for anybody in the state of nature who is involved in a contract.

Hobbes' politics were meant to be practical and for this world - he was no idealist. His answer to the Foole is common-sense: perhaps especially in war we have need for confederates. Competitively successful confederations are those which (amongst other things) have a high degree of internal co-operation and cohesion. We can now see easily how the answer to the Foole goes some distance towards undermining the supposed need for instituting the commonwealth. If that is true, the state of nature is not necessarily an unmitigated disaster. In fact we, and Hobbes, might be able to do quite a lot with it (perhaps in it?). But there might be a rub here: true, it is rational (Hobbes' sense of the term) to keep one's promises in the state of nature. Unfortunately there are enough fools (irrational souls) about, bent on satisfying short-term gains in partiality, pride and revenge, to upset the stability of voluntary co-operation. And, the objection might go on, the real common-sense in Hobbes is demonstrated in the institution of sovereign power. The only stable, reliable form of co-operation there is ever likely to be has to have force to back it up because of the incidence of foolishness.

Actually, the implications are not that straightforward. On the one hand we have the seed of an idea from Hobbes himself: being in need of confederates in the state of nature, it is prudentially rational to keep "covenants made". On the other hand, it could be that humans - enough of them, anyway - are so incorrigibly dim-witted when it comes to handling their long-term interests that they must have these managed for them (by the sovereign). Notice that, at the time of its inception, the state is not a remedy for irrationality,[8] it merely works to suppress its manifestation. Until the tendency to be irrational can be turned around (by education or indoctrination, say - both longish-term projects) it is held in check by threats, offers or throffers, to use Taylor's (1982) terms. As controls on behaviour, these measures are effective if those subject to them have at least a prudential sense of consequences. Theoretically there is an issue here: is it not true that the cognitive requirements for working out how to behave to realise long-term benefits in a statist community are exactly the same as those, for the same reasons, in a state of nature confederacy? In which case is it not possible that a state of nature confederacy is at least as politically possible as a sovereign commonwealth? It is this third possibility, which has emerged from the analysis of Hobbes' argument, that now attracts attention.

The commonwealth and a state of nature confederation are similar in one important respect. Their ends are the same: to maintain enough peace for people to pursue their PI interests. The difference between them is that, in the former, the contractors agree to trade off some of their natural rights to self-government for peace; no such commitment is necessarily required in a confederation (albeit prudence counsels against intemperate exercise of natural rights). In other words, the difference is one of means, not ends. So how could the peace be maintained, without the sword, in a state of nature confederacy? The language of game theory is by now very familiar and besides provides a convenient shorthand. I shall use it for purposes of brevity here, especially since the "moves", and the reasons for them, are very PIst. There is no suggestion that I might be essaying any game theoretic debate; on the contrary I simply follow the conventions as used by Taylor (1987) in his *The Possibility of Co-operation*. We start with two players P1 and P2 who contract with each other. In a one-play game, if P1 reneges then so too does P2. The result is Pareto-inferior (had both co-operated the result would have been Pareto-optimal). This is the standard reading of how Hobbes understood the state of nature. However, in his answer to the

Foole, P1 having played C (co-operated), P2 should do the same, otherwise P1 will fall back on the escape clause (the second clause of the first law of nature) and thus actualise that state of "warre" which jeopardises P2's possession not only of her ill-gotten gains but of liberty and life as well. Of course this is not necessarily an argument which will discourage P2 from playing D (default or renege; I take these as synonyms); she might think P1 is a puny threat. But a bipartite, one-play game is nothing like akin to our experience.

Much more familiar to us is a multiple play game with no players having a reliable means to predict which will be the last play. The sub-clause is obviously important: if the multiple play game is a finite set and the last game known to both players, the final result would be exactly the same as a single play game. And, closer still to the usual would be a game with more than two players. There might be P1 ... Pn, though not all of whom are playing each other simultaneously: P1 might be playing P3 at the time when P2 is playing P4, and so on. The logic of this is transparent enough though one feature might be worth emphasising. Agreed, if P1 and P2 were the only players in an iterated game, playing C,C optimises and D,D must become a fatuous exercise in time; but it is not quite the same in an iterated multi-player game. Quite the reverse: if P1 plays P3 for the first time, then D has the best pay-off. And this holds good ... so long as each play is a one-off and discrete. However, the reality of social life is different. Each time, say, P3 plays D to another's C, the stock of "bitten" players goes up. Two factors follow: firstly, bitten players, no matter who they are playing, are going to drive harder, tighter bargains, e.g. insist on playing second in some crucial aspect of the deal and, secondly, known default gamesters are going to attract some notoriety. People do talk about each other, after all, and in the interests of self-protection, they build up an inventory of those they can trust and of those whose probity is open to question. To the extent that P3, in our example, finds herself on more and more inventories of the untrustworthy by so much does she find herself excluded from further games and, therefore, the benefits of play.[9] Thus, what began with Hobbes' answer to the Foole turns out to have a wider implication: a state of nature confederation of PIs, engaged in an iterated, multiple play game of trading goods is possible. Possible in that it is not doomed by its structure to collapse into self-defeating anarchy; rather, it has built-in strategies for excluding free riders (e.g. P3) from the benefits of confederation.

What I have suggested, thus far, is that on Hobbes' own PI terms he admits three political options, not two:

(a)   the state of nature as self-defeating anarchy,
(b)   states, social contract derived and
(c)   state of nature confederations.

(a) and (b) are overtly treated in *Leviathan*; (c) is suggested. However, if the implications from that suggestion are teased out in more detail than Hobbes wished or dared to, we discover the possibility of a society which can be co-operative without it being essential to have a specialism in coercive government to achieve this. Of course it is ironical that the idea for this is gathered from Hobbes' second argument against the Foole which is apparently directed against those who would seriously consider reneging on their act of institution of the sovereign. Nevertheless, the opening for (c) is there because it is essential that the voluntary and co-operative act of institution takes place in the state of nature. This implies that the need for the coercive commonwealth is theoretically redundant. And that opens up three possibilities, depending on from where we begin. Firstly, suppose there is a state. Though Hobbes (1968, p.260) sometimes says that no matter how bad it is - bad in its treatment of subjects, bad in management, whatever - it cannot be as bad as the misery of the state of nature, yet that no longer follows. People disaffected with the state can use the escape clause and have a chance of improving their expectations. Thus, anarchic revolution is a practical option for Hobbesians. Secondly, suppose there is no state, then, as I have just said, (b) or (c) are equally genuine choices for (c) is not identical with (a). Furthermore, PIs, such as Hobbes takes people to be, might very well prefer (c) to (b). And, thirdly, coming out of the second, Hobbes' contemporary critics were quite right: his consent to (b) is conditional; the sovereign retains government subject to being able to keep the peace (as a convenience to subjects to pursue their own ends).

In this chapter I hope to have shown how Hobbes anticipated two key arguments in subsequent anarchist philosophy: that people might not wish there to be states and, if they do not, they are not stuck with Hobson's Choice in the matter. Anarchy is a political option, from which it follows that political philosophy is indeed not limited in scope to working out the respective rights and duties of governed and government. Furthermore, Hobbes manages this with a fixed dispositional structure of possessive individualism and its consequential value orderings. That is no mean achievement in that it is commonly supposed that it is because of the PI streak in us that we must have states.

Modest progress has been achieved so far: the PI predicament does not make the state necessary. However, it could still be objected that, though PIs might prefer the state of nature, yet they will be better off in states. In the next chapter a vigorous anarchic reply to that challenge will be considered. The idea is to see how PIs, in possession of full-blooded natural rights, might manage in the state of nature. The success or otherwise of this endeavour should give us a clearer idea of the direction anarchy can take, if any.

Notes

1 Note, however, it is part of the task in this chapter to explain that it is not actually Hobson's Choice.
2 But see Strauss, L. (1952), *The Political Philosophy of Hobbes*, Oxford: Oxford University Press.
3 Here and throughout, Taylor's and Nozick's understanding of coercion is followed, viz.:

> ... successfully making credible, substantial threats. For a threat to be coercive it must bring about compliance and it must do this by proposing a sanction which the recipient expects to be imposed in the event of non-compliance and which makes the non-compliant action (together with the imposition of the sanction) substantially less attractive than the compliant action (without the sanction). (Taylor, 1982, p.14)

4 See chapters 2 and 3, below, for a contrast between Nozick and Rothbard on this point.
5 See, e.g. Peters, R.S. (1967), *Hobbes*, Penguin: Harmondsworth.
6 Or five, if we subscribe to Warrender's interpretation, see Warrender, H. (1957), *The Political Philosophy of Hobbes: his Theory of Obligation*, Oxford: Clarendon Press.

7   Legitimacy, as a rich moral consideration, does not have to come into the matter of support for government. This is obviously true in cases where government - and para-government agencies - force some people into a state of nature even though the victims have no criminal or political case to answer. This can happen and the general level of support for the government increase, e.g. in the case of victimising a (mistrusted) minority.

8   Although, in fairness to Hobbes, he said it is an important job for government to educate subjects into a proper understanding of its role in keeping the peace.

9   I shall build up on this idea, working it into a process of ostracism which is an effective means of social control in acephalous societies. See chapters 3 and 6, below.

2 Possessive individualists in libertarian anarchy

Acephalous confederations are not equivalent to self-defeating anarchy, it was argued in chapter 1. And it is possible that PIs might choose not to live in states. That, by itself, is no argument for anarchy. So what is? That question is the pre-occupation of this chapter. Here a beginning will be made where, in one sense, we left Hobbes, i.e. with PI psychology and natural rights. In this chapter consideration will be given to how far these components, by themselves, can take us towards practical anarchy. On the face of it, working with PI dispositions plus natural rights, and nothing besides, is working with very few tools yet self-styled libertarian anarchists hold they are quite enough. They argue that with them, in a state of nature, we can build an economic structure which will support anarchic society. Now, firstly, I shall outline a comprehensive model of libertarian anarchy. Secondly, attention will be drawn to an aspect of the dynamics of libertarian economics which actually runs counter to its normative ambitions. This will indicate either (a) a need for a state (the subject of chapter 3) or (b) a revised normative perspective (the subject of chapter 5).

Murray Rothbard, a libertarian anarchist, writes:

> One of the most commonly derided constructions of classical economic theory is "Crusoe Economics", the analysis of an isolated man face-to-face with nature. And yet, this seemingly "unrealistic"

18

model, ..., has highly important and even indispensable uses. It serves to isolate man as against nature, thus gaining clarity by abstracting from the beginning from inter-personal relationships. Later on, this man/nature analysis can be extended and applied to the "real world". The bringing in of "Friday", or of one or more other persons, after analysis of strictly Robinsonian isolation, then serves to show how the addition of other persons affects the discussion. These conclusions can then also be applied to the contemporary world. Thus, the abstraction of analyzing a few persons interacting on an island enables a clear perception of the basic truths of interpersonal relations, truths which remain obscure if we insist on looking first at the contemporary world only whole and of a piece. If Crusoe economics can and does supply the indispensable groundwork for the entire structure of economics and praxeology - the broad, formal analysis of human action - a similar procedure should be able to do the same thing for social philosophy, for the analysis of the fundamental truths of the nature of man vis-a-vis the nature of the world into which he is born as well as the world of other men. Specifically, it can aid greatly in solving such problems of political philosophy as the role and nature of liberty. (1982, p.29)

Rothbard believes that one of the most misguided suppositions in archic thought is that human nature is deficient, requiring external controls upon it in order to protect its long-term interests. On the contrary, he says, human nature fits into a universal pattern, natural law, where everything has its particular - but not deficient - form and place. For instance, it is part of human nature that:

... each individual person *must,* in order to act, choose his own ends and employ his own means in order to attain them ... Since men can think, feel, evaluate, and act only as individuals, it becomes vitally necessary for each man's survival and prosperity that he be free to learn, choose, develop his faculties and act upon his knowledge and values. (1973, p.26, italics added)

Interference with this independent process is "profoundly antihuman; it violates the natural law of man's needs". And human needs, as he has promised, Rothbard articulates with his Crusoe social philosophy.

19

Imagine Crusoe *in situ* on the island but amnesiac. What does he "confront"? Firstly, he is an embodied consciousness, with needs and desires, who discovers himself in a land provided with some resources. Lacking instincts which will propel him automatically towards the means for needs satisfaction, he is thrown back on what his cognitive capacities can work out about the island's resources if he is to survive. When he utilises this knowledge Crusoe transforms the naturally occurring resources into consumables. With these he satisfies, first, his basic need for food and, second, his additional want for the food to be more palatable. In the cases of both needs and wants, "Crusoe must *produce* before he can *consume*" (p.30). He discovers what his needs and wants are by "introspection" and how to satisfy them by "extrospection" (p.31). Two awarenesses gathered from introspection are that he has "inviolable and inalienable" free will and "natural ownership over himself" (p.31). Natural ownership has ramifications to which we shall return presently.

Before that, however, imagine Crusoe again, on this occasion deliberating: shall he eat the berries or the mushrooms which are before him? He decides upon the mushrooms. On the point of eating them a stranger bursts upon the scene shouting, "Don't do that! Those mushrooms are poisonous". This introduces the basis for Rothbard's evaluative scheme. Poison is descriptively injurious to health. Extrapolating: what promotes an organism's health and life is good for it; what favours pain and death, bad.[1] The moral objectivity at issue here is not disinterested. On the contrary, it is limited to first person reference. So, though you must look after *your* health, you are not required to concern yourself with mine. It follows, we are told (1973, p.32), that if Crusoe persists in eating the mushrooms, knowing them to be poisonous, his act is "objectively immoral".

The island is unowned, since it is "unused and uncontrolled", when Crusoe arrives. As he transforms its resources into utilities, when he "mixes his labor with the soil", he converts them into his property (p.33). In other words, for isolated agents, their property is defined as those resources they have used, transformed or otherwise have control over. Consequently, claiming as property an entity over which one has no control is "vainglory", an articulation without significance.

We now move further into the issue of property by considering circumstances where people of various skills produce different things. These things, if their surplus is exchanged, increase material benefits to those who trade them (all going according to plan). Exchange can be done variously. It is at this point that Rothbard seeks to show that one method of exchange - free market capitalism - is altogether superior to its major alternative, property collectivism.

Consider the perspective of those who favour collectivist means of production and distribution of goods. Those inclined to this view object to the free market on the grounds of it being unfair: those who are poorly resourced or otherwise relatively weak trading partners are at the mercy of stronger bargainers. Being strong is not a *justification* for taking advantage of the weak. Quite the reverse, this trading relationship is unjust. Rothbard responds to this challenge with alacrity. He adopts (1973, p.36) Ricardo's Law of Comparative Advantage to the effect that, in the free market, the weak achieve advantages because it benefits the strong to exchange with them. The example to illustrate the law is of a physician who employs a secretary. Even though the medic is better at secretarial tasks than the employee, he retains the secretary because he wants to keep his time free for "far more productive work". Contrary to the fears of egalitarian collectivists, the free market provides benefits to weaker trading partners because the stronger can afford to buy what (little) they have to offer.[2] If Ricardo's Law holds, the free market cannot be rejected on the grounds of it being economically unfair. To this we shall return in the critical section of this chapter.

Exchange is not of goods, *per se*, but in ownership rights over them. Ownership rights include absolute determination over consumption, further transformation and disposal. The most primitive form of exchange is barter, meat for eggs, metals for timber, etc. A much more adaptable and efficient economy can be generated, however, when there is a common medium for exchange; some commodity, such as gold, for instance, will serve the purpose. As the trading network expands (Crusoe is now dealing with Friday and an indefinite number of other traders), the common medium - money - becomes practically indispensable insofar as so much more trading can be achieved with it for:

> Within a barter system, there is great inconvenience and cost to searching for someone who has what you want and wants what you have, even in a market place ... (Nozick, 1974, p.18)

Money makes the mark of worth common and generally applicable irrespective of the particular character of the transaction. But, though money makes trade easier, it does not alter fundamental economics: wealth is always generated by the transformation of resources into products or the sale of labour. At the same time economics can, and does, become a little more elaborate. Take the idea of "vertical" exchange, for instance, which ushers in the middleman and wage-labourer:

1   A produces goods x.
2   C wants x.
3   But it is not easy (cost efficient) to transport x from A to C.
4   B, however, specialises as a go-between for such as A and C.
5   B buys x (for A).
6   And employs D and E to transport x from A to C.
7   On arrival at C's, B sells x to C.
8   Her price covers costs (purchase price from A + D & E's wages) and leaves her a profit.
9   Whereas A, B and C successively will have owned x, D and E never have.
10 But D and E have gained by exchanging their labour for wages from B.

In sum, B is a capitalist, one who risks capital by buying from A on the chance (calculated to be a good one) of gaining on the sale to C. B's employment of D and E saves them the need to be risk takers or asset savers before they can be consumers.

Here it might be interjected: what really happens to D and E is that they are alienated from control of production; is that not a form of denial of their Crusoe rights? Not at all, is the reply:

... the indispensable and enormously important function of [B] the capitalist ... is to save the laborers from the necessity of restricting their consumption and thus saving up the capital themselves, and from waiting for their pay until the product would (...) be sold at a profit further down the chain of production. Hence the capitalist, far from somehow depriving the laborer of his rightful ownership of the product, makes possible a payment to the laborer considerably in advance of the sale of the product. Furthermore, the capitalist, in his capacity as forecaster ... saves the laborer from the risk that the product might not be sold at a profit, or that he might even suffer losses. (Rothbard, 1973, p.39)

Moreover, the free market (1-10, above) is "a society of voluntary *and consequently* mutually beneficial exchanges of ownership titles between specialized producers" (p.40). He equates (p.41) the free market with "free society" or, sometimes, "pure liberty" which, we remind ourselves, is "founded on the basic natural facts of man: each individual's ownership by his ego over his own person and his own labor, and his ownership over the land resources which he finds and transforms". So long as this ownership and the free market are not "molested", loss of freedom is *not* a price humans have to pay for civilization.[3]

There are two more aspects to the libertarian case which are needed for discussion purposes, viz. (i) the understanding of coercion in general and sanctions in particular and (ii) the rejection of the legitimacy of the state.

Coercion (1973, p.45) is a form of aggression and "What such aggressive violence means is that one man *invades* the property of another without the victim's consent" and frustrates the latter's "freely adopted ideas and values, and ... actions based on such values" (1982, p.46). Specific to the present topic, parasitism (which is generally referred to as free riding elsewhere in this book) is a form of aggression and has the additional, consequential negative effect of reducing the stock of production (in a fixed sum, as the number of parasites on production rises, the number of producers decreases). However, not all acts of aggression are illegitimate, only those which violate property are. It follows (p.59) that the actions of (statist) governments are illegitimate insofar as they invade property (by taxation) without their victims' consent. All states (1973, p.49) have this characteristic in common which make them criminal organisations, that is they all contravene our inalienable natural rights which Rothbard (1973, p.47) draws together in what he calls the libertarian creed:[4]

(a) the unconditional moral priority of individuals' property rights in their persons and objects they have voluntarily acquired and
(b) the concomitant rejection of any right to trespass on (a).

Libertarians reject the claim that there is a *bona fide* exchange - taxes in exchange for protection - between states and governed on the grounds that there is no deal and, indeed, there cannot be, so long as the governed are compelled to pay taxes. That compulsion remains theft.

So, suppose for argument's sake, we have espoused libertarianism. Believing states are irredeemably wicked, we have disposed of them. All very well but for the fact that free riders are also bad ... and are still with us. At least when there were states we had means of curtailing - if not eradicating - the activities of free riders. This, of course, is the prudential objection *manqué* which anarchist advocates must rebut.

Libertarians anticipate Nozick in their reply: protection and rights enforcement are offered on a fee-for-service basis in the free market. The system is not perfect, e.g. conflicts between adjacent police agencies might erupt from time to time, but we can afford to be phlegmatic about such imperfections. In the first place, whatever harm is caused by inter-agency disagreements will be minuscule in comparison to the havoc wrought by statist wars. Secondly, protection, as a business operation, embodies certain sensible restrictions. For instance, what Rothbard delicately calls "noisy protection" is bad for business - customers are not comforted by the spectacle of their agents blazing away at each other. It is in the best self-interests of agencies to settle their differences quietly. They can conveniently do this by referring their contentions to another business, third-person arbitration. Private arbitration already enjoys considerable success in actuality and there is evidence (1973, pp.229-30) of it being used in preference to statist jural systems when it is on offer. Of course, arbitrators do not have the right to impose violent penalties on persons but they may justly require of them that they compensate for property damage done. Failure to comply with this requirement results in boycott or ostracism.[5] Uniformity of legal principles and derivative codes will be secured under a universal commitment to the libertarian creed though, as a matter of commonsense, there will have to be worked out some rules of evidence - common law will do very well for that purpose.

To sum up: in spirit and deed libertarian anarchy is regarded by its champions as the most congenial, if not only, social environment for possessive individualists (which supposedly we all are). And there is a very plausible sense in which we could say they elevate Hobbes' escape clause to the standing of a moral imperative.

I now discuss two possibilities. Firstly, that the extreme individualism and normative sparsity of this anarchy endangers its own survival. Secondly, that the first point might render some sort of state - possibly a minimal state, to foreshadow Nozick - a practical necessity.

Rothbard has two figures with which he gives concrete illustrations of his argumentative points. One we have met already: Crusoe. Another is the homesteader, the person who settles on some vacant land, works it and thereby makes it his own and his source of livelihood. Imagine, now, homesteaders A and B. Each had off-spring; A one child, A1, and B ten, B1...B10. Spouses are of no account here - they died long before the story begins. The story opens with the deaths of A and B who leave their respective properties to their children. A1 is the sole beneficiary in A's will and B's estate is divided up equally between B1...B10. A's and B's holdings were of equal size, thus we might expect A1's inheritance to be ten times greater than that of any of the Bs. But, as things turn out, any 1/10 of A1's property is more valuable than the inheritances of B1...B10. After years of over-cultivation, attempting to produce sufficient to feed the prodigious family, B's land is played out and yields less per acre with each season. In the course of time, the B children fall below a subsistence standard of living. A1, having the capital reserves to buy all the B land, restore it and turn it to profit, puts a proposal to each of B1...B10: he will buy their pieces and employ them to work on his augmented estates, called A+ Holdings. Even if the purchase price is modest, so long as the wages equal at least the present nett returns on their allotments, B1...B10 are better off if they accept A1's offers (a case of Rothbard's use of Ricardo's Law). They accept the offers. Rothbardian PIs will applaud presumably, because all, so far, is consistent with the libertarian creed and the operations of the free market. But, later, with the B children all working for him, A1 cuts their wages (and, as a matter of fact, there is no alternative paid employment available to them). To begin with they can make ends meet by drawing on their savings, the money A1 paid them for their land. True, B1...B10 were at liberty to decline to accept the pay cut and quit A+ Holdings but, with no alternative means of providing for themselves there is Hobson's Choice in the matter (starvation is a degree worse than poverty). Depending on the extent to which A1 wishes to maximise profits by reducing his wages bill, he can introduce the refinement called the Company Store (obviously a subsidiary of A+ Holdings). Here his employees, short of cash, can buy on credit (at whatever the asking price - they are in no position to question it). The workers are now in debt to A+ Holdings so it keeps their wages back to pay off some of the debts. It is a good idea for A1 to always keep the workers in some debt (high profit margins on goods sold in the Store easily offset these outstanding debts) because, in order to not "violate" his rights, they are then morally obliged to continue to work for him.

By this stage B1...B10 are malnourished and poorly clothed *yet* A1 has not broken a bargain with them (at the time of his offers nothing was mentioned about *future* wages fluctuating) or stolen from them. In sum, there has been no violation of the libertarian creed. To use Rothbard's phrase, there is nothing "objectively immoral" in A1's conduct. However, if any of the B family were to pilfer from A1 that *would* be contrary to the creed and, quite justly, penalisable (e.g. B1, the thief, may be obliged to "work off" the value of the goods she stole). Elsewhere[6] I have called the relationship which now exists between A1 and his employees, including B1...B10, the "peon relationship", after the stark paradigm of the owner-labourer relations in the silver mines in Colombia.[7] Since there will be occasion to refer to this same pattern of economic relations on future occasions I will take advantage of the brevity by referring to it as the peon relationship from here on.

Suppose the peon relationship intensifies: B1...B10 are distressed to the limits of endurance and A1 does nothing, and will do nothing, to ameliorate their condition. In which case, having reached the end of their tether, the Bs must do something - though what can they do that will not violate A1's rights? Consider:

1   They could leave A+ Holdings. This is their most passive option. But, owing money to the Company Store, it molests A1's property rights.
2   They might steal food and clothing from A1. Again a violation of his rights.
3   Or they might rise up and seize A+ Holdings, capturing and/or killing A1 and his agents if need be. This, their most active option, is a complete sack of A1's natural rights, a wholesale desecration of the libertarian creed.

The Bs are caught in what we might call an ethical/practical paradox, viz. they still formally retain their natural rights; their rights are even respected in as much as nobody has violated their persons or other property. At the same time these rights, indeed their whole moral circumstance, are insubstantial, undermined by the fact that they have no means of alleviating their misery which does not "molest" A1's natural rights. The paradox is that their practical options for doing something about the objective moral fact of their poor condition are unethical by the standards of the libertarian creed.[8]

Further, there are similarities between the peon relationship and the case of Hobbes' subjects confronting their sovereign. Whereas option 1, above, is a bit iffy in this regard, 2 and 3 - especially 3 - have all the appearance of being instances of invoking Hobbes' escape clause. The difference between the two cases has a certain irony about it: Hobbes' escape clause is used by people who cannot "win" in the state; the Bs (or peons) use options 2 and 3 to escape what has become for them self-defeating anarchy. Apart from appreciating the irony, that datum is to be put to one side for a moment. More immediately and argumentatively important is to recall that a few pages earlier I foreshadowed a discussion about the normative sparsity of libertarian anarchism. The moment is opportune for that. It was argued, in chapter 1 and elsewhere,[9] that Hobbes had far greater depth of moral and political understanding than many, if not most, of his critics have given him credit for. One might go further: libertarians, such as Rothbard, though they eschew him in their work, would nevertheless benefit their arguments had they done otherwise. Hobbes, we know, subscribed to natural rights theory and the general psychology of PIsm. In that he is in concert with libertarians. However, he takes the laws of nature to be moral imperatives; in that he differs from Rothbard who takes them to be descriptive. So, to return to the peon relationship. Faced with its predicament, if the Bs were Hobbesians it would be legitimate for them to use the escape clause - required of them, really. Nobody may licitly, directly or indirectly, compel others to go without the necessities for physical well being; the very attempt to do so is enough to provoke the would-be victim into using the escape clause. A1's treatment of B1...B10 has resulted in their being ill-clothed and under-nourished - deprivation of some of the necessities for physical well being. It follows that they may, indeed, choose any one of options 1, 2 or 3 - in the long-term 3, if it works, produces the best results for them for, obviously, A1 ceases to be a menace in their lives. The libertarian argument under discussion does not have the escape clause; that is, not in Hobbes' form. Of course libertarians should resort to "warre" if their property is invaded. But, to reiterate, in the peon relationship their property is not invaded. At the same time the peons' relationship to their employer makes their lives intolerable. Hobbes appreciated that PI natural rights holders can be damaged as much by neglect as attack and they ought to be allowed to protect themselves from both. Libertarians place themselves in a more vulnerable position. From "equal opportunity" the free market can produce unequal outcomes of such a magnitude that some people have no hope whatsoever of benefit from libertarian anarchy.[10] Politically, that renders this form of anarchy endemically unreliable for, when the peon relationship does develop, the peons have no practical choice but Hobbes' escape clause. It follows that, contrary to Rothbard's hopes, the free market is not always best and most congenial for all concerned. And if the precedent after which the relationship is named is anything to go by, the free market could well degenerate into *tyranny*. Consider, for instance: the peons are becoming desperate and, sometimes, dangerous. Many are resorting to option 2 followed promptly by 1, replete with proceeds of 2. Others are using 2 and giving serious thought to 3;[11] isolated cases of violence are already increasing. Evidently A1 must buy more and more "protection" for his property against these occurrences. The guards will certainly be encouraged to work with vigour and enthusiasm. Private property and personal liberty might well be reconcilable but not necessarily so in the free market. (For the moment, A1's option of *improving* labour conditions is put to one side. As a PI, A1 *could* try that as a measure to secure increased productivity but he is in no wise obliged to ... and it is with his moral position that we are interested here.)

In a moment I wish to give attention to a difficulty for the free market in the matter of conflicting rights claims. But, *a propos* the discussion so far, it is interesting to note that there is a theoretical solution to Rothbard's difficulty to be found in much earlier work in the individualist anarchist tradition (from which I take libertarianism to be a modern growth). Josiah Warren's (Miller, 1984, ch.3) idea of "equitable commerce" would, if practicable, *forestall* the emergence of the peon relationship. Warren advocated that goods be exchanged for the cost of production (= labour time [+ "repugnance" in the nature of the work, if necessary]). Quite deliberately Warren excluded profit from licit exchange. In small communities, of farmers, artisans and professionals in a modest way, the general economic momentum would be towards equality of wealth. However Warren was no economic romantic, looking back fondly to simpler days. He recognised a place in the economy for industrialised means of production, e.g. A+ Holdings. The difference between his industry and Rothbard's is that he insisted A1 may not extract more in the way of returns from A+ Holdings than he pays B1...B10. I shall come back to the role played by rough equality of economic outcomes in chapters 6 and 7. For the present it is mentioned by way of indicating that one does not have to move away from the individualist perspective on anarchy to realise that there are self-stabilising mechanisms within it which are really quite simple. Thinking back on the Crusoe economics: was there any argumentative need to build in a profit factor? No; its appearance, though permissible, was not claimed to be necessary. If not essential then, by its omission, a problem is dissolved.

Thus far it has been argued that there are serious practical dangers in following the libertarian formula (viz., natural rights + capital economics = the good life). Notwithstanding the foregoing, it is still open to possessive individualists of a libertarian persuasion to insist that any morally permissible society must have an unconditional respect for property rights. One question then is: will circumstances be such that this requirement can always be met?

Libertarian natural rights, let us be in no doubt about this, are universal and, since there is no other necessary moral dimension - a deontology, for instance - we can expect they have to carry considerable normative weight. Can they? Take the example of (another) would-be homesteader who happens upon a piece of land with nobody on it and uncultivated. The homesteader works it, in all honesty believing, as a Crusoe economist, he has made the first claim upon it. Sometime later, a party of Red Indians arrives. The Indians are angry to discover the homesteader has killed their game, grubbed out their edible root and fruit bearing plants and, to cap it all, tells them they are trespassing on his land.[12] For their part, the Indians insist the homesteader has violated their rights to this land which they include in their hunter/gatherer domain. To be sure, they have left no obvious signs of their occupancy, of having "mixed their labour" with the land but, after all, they are not farmers. They are nomads, using this tract according to its seasonal advantages. Nonetheless they claim, genuinely enough on Rothbard's terms, to have indeed controlled and produced from their resource by their hunting its game and harvesting the plants in order to provision themselves.

Both parties appear to have conducted themselves quite properly as property right holders. Certainly there appears no clear-cut case to be made against either for illegitimate appropriation. At any rate thus it might seem to an arbitrator. (It is assumed that the homesteader and the Indians have taken their case to one such.) Nevertheless there is, patently, a rights dispute on hand. Suppose the arbitrator says the land belongs to the Indians by virtue of precedent occupancy. In which case, since the homesteader has already invested labour in the land he could - should - claim compensation for his loss of goods. But then the Indians cannot legitimately be required to pay compensation because there is no case for saying people should be paid for working one's property when they were not asked to in the first place. Furthermore, they lodge the counter-claim that this so-called work was a violation of their property - just look at the damage done! If anything the homesteader should be paying them in full measure for his molesting their property. Both parties have equally legitimate but mutually contradicting property molestation claims. A putative third option available to the arbitrator is to suggest a compromise, e.g. the Indians take half the disputed land, the homesteader the other. Yet this move fares no better than the others. Both parties, being possessive individuals, will, by disposition, reject this and are not obliged, in any moral sense to hand, to accept a loss of 50% of their property. A fourth option is to settle the matter on chance - the toss of a coin, say - and the winner takes all. Again, there is nothing in hand to say the parties should play hazard for what is already theirs. Now there might well be resolutions to this conflict but, on the basis of libertarian rights alone, they do not appear to be accessible.[13] We cannot satisfy the inalienable property rights of both claims yet they are both legitimate. The situation libertarians are faced with here replicates that confronted by the peon-relationship at least to this extent: the creed allows a situation to develop which is contrary to its aspirations - not to mention those of a number of people caught up in it - but which, on its own terms, it cannot handle. In both cases, solutions to the problem are to be sought *outside* the libertarian brief.

That, of course, is not a reason for turning away altogether from the libertarian path. All that has been shown so far is that libertarian PI ethical naturalism, in conjunction with its economics, is not a reliable route to practical, sustainable anarchy. At the same time it might be possible, with some adjustments, to turn it to some constructive effect. I have suggested that the adjustments will be found off the Rothbardian agenda. But, in all fairness, I might be wrong here. Rothbard discusses the character of anarchic law at considerable length though, as yet, no mention has been made of it here. Before one can say the peons, the homesteader and the Indians are beyond help from him, one had better attend to his legal constructions. Then, and only then, will the three strands of his anarchy, i.e. its ethics, economics and social control system have been canvassed.

Libertarians, in company with most anarchists, accept that security and public order are necessary conditions for the good life. And, in the same company, they claim both can be provided in their preferred version of acephalous society. What gives libertarian anarchy its distinctive character is, first, the requirement that all security and public order procedures be congruent with the libertarian creed; all legal actions are actions about property rights. There is historical evidence to substantiate the claim for the practicality and actuality of civil law requiring no state enforcement. Rothbard cites the *filid* law of Ancient Ireland, common law, mercantile and admiralty law, all of which developed in response to regulative needs and independently of states (for all that, subsequently, some were absorbed into state legal codes). Besides, even in modern states not all law, or law-like processes, are state controlled. There exist private systems of arbitration. Second, libertarian legal thinking differs from modern state criminal codes in that the former believes where there is no plaintiff, accusing another party of rights violation, there is no cause. It follows there are no victimless crimes, such as narcotics use, for anarchists of this persuasion. Third, to keep faith with the libertarian creed, judgements and penalties cannot violate the liberty rights of tortfeasors by imposing arrest, incarceration or bodily harm upon them. So, what forms may penalties take and how shall they be effected? Noted already is that property violations are to be paid for by their perpetrators; property is forfeit to make good the damage. This is backed-up with threats of boycott and ostracism should there be non-compliance - and, when executed, both these are potent measures. Boycott, for instance, will ruin a business and ostracism deprives the victim of all the benefits of human society.[14]

The bipartite construction of legal cause is too simple, it has been said in criticism of libertarian law. What is to be done, for instance, for third parties who are affected by the matter being tried? The bipartite system appears to have no room for them. Wierk's (1978, p.219) example

31

is that of a plumber who has done some faulty work in a house which the landlord, who commissioned the work, leases. Whereas the landlord can, but, say, does not sue the plumber, what is to become of the tenants whose lives are affected by the faulty work? The building is not their property so they have no legal standing in the matter. It is doubtful, though, that this objection is successful. Rothbard could make short work of it: the tenants, who have suffered creature discomfort as a result of the plumber's activities, can bring an action against him for violating their (bodily) rights. They are entitled to do this quite independently of the landlord's decision.

Another objection is that, in the case where the number of plaintiffs is very large, the libertarian legal process will become hopelessly inefficient. Stone (1978, p.211) has the example where harm is large in aggregate "but diffused among many victims". Imagine, say, one million people suffer $100 each worth of damages from pollution arising out of the activities of one factory. Because there is no provision for a "class action" in Rothbard, the process of law here has the promise of being very clumsy, frustrating and time consuming - all the parties involved might be long dead before the millionth claim could come to trial! Again, however, Rothbard's notion of legal activity is not badly damaged. In this case, there is no need for there to be a million actions for $100 to be processed. The simplest thing would be for the million people with a grievance to take their matter to the same protection agency, argue it as a corporate interest and, if successful, disperse the damages to each individual at the rate of $100 each. This might seem an odd way of settling legal benefits but it is quite common in gambling circles. For instance, a group of people buys several tickets in a lottery so as to increase the odds on one of their tickets winning. When that actually happens, the group then divides up the prize equally.

Critical attempts, such as the above, take state legal operations as paradigms of just process and, by implication, find departures from it wanting. But that does not follow. Real trouble with private law, in libertarian hands, comes from a wrap-around connection with its economics. Rothbard believes that the competitive nature of the free market will countervail the emergence of monopolies. That belief has been disputed here, particularly with the example of the peon relationship. Now, let Rothbard be taken at face value: the legal system is available on fee-for-service terms. It is agreed that this will render it no more venal than statist systems; perhaps a little less - crooked courts might not long survive their bad name. Maybe so. But courts can be bought and sold, just as any other commodity. Suppose there are three courts in town: Smith's, Jones' and Brown's, and, naturally, they are in competition. The competition between them might very well conduce to their customers being given good value for money. However, the capital economic phenomenon of undercutting does tend towards monopoly formation and occurs frequently, though Rothbard gives it scant regard. So when Smith's has undercut, forced out of business, then bought up the assets of Jones and Brown at bargain prices, it might very well control the entire town's arbitrators, lawyers, police and insurance agencies. Smith's has become what Nozick (1974) will call a Dominant Protective Agency with interests neither more nor less altruistic than A1 and A+ Holdings. Whereas Nozick, it will be noted, propounds "moral side-constraints" with which to temper the extremes of possessive individualism, free market libertarianism does not - a point already made much of in discussing the peon relationship. This is where the wrap-around occurs. A legal system, understood as a form of behavioural regulator could, in principle, restrain PIsm from becoming raw egoism of the calibre demonstrated by A1 but to achieve that there *has* to be a normative ingredient other than the libertarian creed. Without it there is no reason why Smith's, the protection monopoly, should not end up like A1, or, perhaps more appropriately, the film anti-hero, Judge Roy Bean.[15] This far from unlikely contingency counts against law being able to temper, let alone prevent, the threat of the peon relationship.

The conclusion to this chapter can be prefaced with a question: who will benefit from "pure liberty" anarchy, as outlined above? The quick answer is: those who do well on the free market. Given equal opportunity that could be anyone. But, I have tried to show, there is no reason to suppose it will be everyone; perhaps, depending on the degree of consolidation by monopolies, it might be very few. And there is no assurance that, as the future becomes present, even those who earnestly aspire to benefit from the free market will. Take the B family: B1 might work very hard to profit from the free market but, in the end, circumstances which he might not have foreseen and, anyway, could not control, close in on him. Those who expect to do well from pure liberty are not equivalent to those who will do well. As to who will depends on countless contingencies. On a prudential calculation alone and quite aside from any more morally rich considerations, *it is rational for individuals to give some probability to ending up at the thin end of the peon relationship*. In which case it is equally rational to consider other options. I repeat, this does not imply a blanket rejection of PI free market anarchy. All it implies is that this form of anarchy is structured with too few normative tools on too narrow a psychological base to be a free-standing political edifice. Unilaterally it will not nurture the degree of morally tempered voluntary co-operation which, I shall go on to argue, a viable acephalous community needs. It is, in an informal sense, a limiting case.

To take stock and seek a way forward: if the purport of this chapter is canvasing what options are available. I have answered: state of nature (such as B1...B10's options 2 and 3) or some independent brake on the development of the peon relationship. The latter promises to cost less, certainly in terms of human suffering and, quite possibly, financially. In chapter 3 that will be considered. To be luminously clear: it will still be assumed that people are dispositionally PI and have fundamental natural rights. The question then is, what must be the character of the independent brake?

Notes

1   Which, of course, is a view in concert with Hobbes' ethical naturalism.
2   In the critical part of this chapter I shall argue that, though the medic/secretary story can be true, it cannot be inferred that, as used by Rothbard, Ricardo's Law is in the least law-like. It will be shown that the labour market can degenerate to a point where the weaker partners are very far from being better off.
3   Bearing in mind Rothbard takes freedom to be of initial opportunity; outcomes are not an issue for him.
4   See also Rothbard, M. (1978), "Society Without a State", in Pennock, J.R. & Chapman, J.W. (eds), *Anarchism*. Nomos xix, p.206.
5   To be mentioned later in this chapter but discussed at greater length in chapters 3-5.
6   Edwards, P. (1985), "The Human Predicament: a Context for Rights & Learning About Rights", *Educational Philosophy & Theory*, Vol.17, pp.38-45.
7   See Pendle, G. (1981), *A History of Latin America*, Harmondsworth: Penguin.

8 Notice, too, that in the peon-relationship the libertarian creed comes into contradiction with the implied Crusoe moral requirement to do that which is beneficial for one's being. Thus, in Crusoe morality the B's should steal from A1 rather than starve and should not steal from him on account of this violating the libertarian creed.

9 See Edwards, J.C.P. (1984), *On the Role of Theism in Hobbes' Political Philosophy*, University of Melbourne, unpublished M.A. thesis.

10 See, too, G.A. Cohen's way of making the same point, *mutatis mutandis*: "... the proletariat is an enslaved class, forced, as a class, to sell its labour power, despite the freedom of many, probably most, of its members not to do so", Cohen, G.A. (1979), "Capitalism, Freedom & the Proletariat", in Ryan, A. (ed), *The Idea of Freedom*, Oxford: Oxford University Press, p.25.

11 Option 2 can, of course, be carried out unilaterally by Pls; there is no need for them to co-operate. On the other hand, to have any realistic hope of success 3 requires at least the voluntary co-operation of a state of nature confederation. That, in turn, is a necessary condition for communitarian anarchy. Thus, the tactics of revolution against libertarian anarchy circumstantially encourage the evolution of community.

12 *Mutatis mutandis*, the example can be re-worked to fit the Crusoe case if, say, Friday is cast as a nomadic hunter/gatherer.

13 One solution would be to compensate from a common purse. In chapter 4 that will be considered further in a general discussion of the functions of Nozick's minimal state. In the present case the arbitrator could reason that (1) the homesteader *unwittingly* violated the Indians' rights, therefore he is not liable to compensate. (2) But the Indians' damage claim is just, so it must be met. (3) The homesteader's work and produce have cash value. (4) Even though (1) implies he should leave, his consequential losses should be redeemed. (5) Therefore pay them both from common insurance stock. This, as will be seen, is very much in tune with Nozick's views.

14 Exactly how almost terrifyingly effective ostracism could be, particularly in the modern world, is illustrated in ch.6, below.

15 From the film *The Life and Times of Judge Roy Bean*, Warner Home Video, 1972.

3 Invisible hand pressures on possessive individualists

A most frequently heard answer to the closing question of chapter 2 is: some sort of state. This is not to say that some form of state is intrinsically good, though it could be. Equally it might be that, social and economic conditions being what they are (at some given time), in nowhere but the state can the distribution of public goods be managed without grotesque differences in receipt occurring. Indeed, so profoundly is this believed by some that the general enterprise of justifying states is considered idle work. The only serious matter in hand for political philosophy is considering what manner of states we ought to have. Williams (1983, p.27) comments in this vein:

> ... one might be prepared to spend time on the justification [of the state] only if one had an idea of some alternative to [it], and it is reasonable to feel that there are, at least now, no real candidates for that.

Falling in with such a presumption is tempting, especially after having considered the predicament anarchy got us into in chapter 2. It might also be misleading. Surely possessive individualists do not have to be Rothbardian libertarians. Indeed they do not. Notwithstanding, there is in the contemporary literature in political philosophy a PI argument, working with very similar presumptive materials to Rothbard's, which states that in even the most favoured anarchic conditions a process of degeneration will occur which will, a fortiori, occasion the state. The argument, if successful, makes the forecast for acephalous society bleak for it claims that anarchy reduces to self-defeating anarchy long before anything as elaborate as the economics of the peon relationship has had time to develop. The case in point is, of course, Robert Nozick's (1974).

In this chapter I propose (a) to lay out Nozick's invisible hand argument for the development of the state, (b) review the extent to which the invisible hand argument is equivocal then (c) take up an historical idea touched on by Rothbard, as a counter-example to Nozick. This idea, the *tuatha* of Ancient Ireland, will be adapted to show how the anarchic state of nature need not degenerate, from which, it will follow, there is no cause for the invisible hand to move society into statehood. The juxtaposition of Nozick's minimal state (MS) with *tuatha* will indicate (d) a conundrum such that if the MS is inescapable it cannot be derived from a "most favourable" anarchic condition (contrary to Nozick's supposition) but if, on the other hand, the MS is not inescapable then it can be shown that the state of nature is preferable to Nozickian PIs.

Contrary to the implied dismissive regard for anarchy as an option detectable in Williams' remark, above, not to mention others, Nozick accords it serious consideration to this extent at least: it cannot be put aside until *argument* shows it to be deficient (morally and/or practically). In *Anarchy, State & Utopia* consideration of the place of anarchy begins from a Lockian outlook upon the state of nature which sees it as beset with certain "inconveniences" for which civil government is the remedy. In reply Nozick (1974, pp.10-11) says:

> To understand precisely what civil government remedies, ... We ... must consider what arrangements might be made within a state of nature to deal with these inconveniences - to avoid them or make them less likely to arise or to make them less serious when they do arise.

At the same time, he goes on to say (p.5), if a state were "superior even to [a] most favoured situation of anarchy" then that would "justify the state".

A most favoured anarchy, or state of nature, (in keeping with Nozick's style these will be taken as synonyms) occurs where "people generally satisfy moral constraints and generally act as they ought" - a "not wildly optimistic" assumption for it does admit of some moral dereliction and backsliding (p.5). Though he will argue that his MS is superior to its "major theoretical" option, anarchy, Nozick (p.5) is careful to emphasise that his postulation of the state of nature really is favourable, going to the extent of contrasting it with a Hobbes-like (but not explicitly Hobbesian) "inevitable process of deterioration" which is analogous to events such as ageing and dying. Moreover, were the state of nature merely a process of deterioration that would not justify the state; it would merely resign us to it as the least awful option.

The material which is to be accommodated by Nozick's political arrangements, whatever they turn out to be, is by now familiar - possessive individualists. People's rights, certain acts of consent to their transference excepting, are inalienable. The rights are to personal (bodily?) non-interference, to possession of private property, of action and association and it is only the like rights of others which "determine the constraints upon [agents'] actions" (p.29). There is "A line (or hyperplane) [which] circumscribes an area in moral space around an individual" (p.57). This line is equivalent to a "boundary" and it is within the boundary that natural rights are located, so to speak. Boundary crossings, in Nozick's phrase, are permissible if certain conditions are met, e.g. if those who cross (and benefit) compensate the subject. Providing transport for epileptics when they are disqualified from driving themselves is one of Nozick's examples of when we ought to compensate for a boundary crossing (= the disqualification from driving). But so riddled with possibilities for dispute are claims of boundary crossings that perhaps (p.74) some "central or unified apparatus capable of making, or entitled to make, these [boundary crossing] decisions" will be required. That, however, is a delicate matter (p.11) for "So strong and far reaching are [agents'] rights that they raise the question of what, if anything, the state and its officials may do".

The main purpose of Nozick's argument is to answer that question. The immediate concern here though is with his prior question: what is there, if anything, in our circumstances which makes the state necessary?

People in the state of nature, it has been said already, usually behave as they ought which means there is general respect for each other's rights. However, in a passage which might just as well have been written in *Leviathan*, Nozick says that in the state of nature the constraint to respect the rights of others is not, in itself, of sufficient

38

force to ensure that *all* people do as they ought. This, coupled with the fact that PIs are disposed to favour their own rights claims, comprise the circumstances which bring about the first invisible hand movement towards the state.[1] There being the occasional moral lapses and deviations, these will ignite normative confrontations between those (possibly) wronged and (possible) wrong-doers. In anarchy all individuals are judges in their own cases but, with their PI bias, they will give themselves the benefit of the doubt. So:

> [People] will overestimate the amount of harm or damage they have suffered, and passions will lead them to attempt to punish others more than proportionately and to exact excessive compensation (...). Thus private and personal enforcement of one's rights (...) leads to feuds, to an endless series of acts of retaliation and exactions of compensation. (p.11)

The implication being, obviously enough, that with anything less than scrupulous fair-mindedness, a disinterested regard for the justice of claims, we will have social decomposition into self-defeating anarchy. That is *unless* there is a "firm way to settle each dispute". Anarchists will accept Nozick's caveat. What they will not accept, because there is nothing they perceive in the logic of the situation which obliges them to, is that the firm way of dispute settlement must be a state, even a minimal state. But that is to anticipate ...

The second move of the invisible hand occurs when, in order to better protect their rights from the odd loose cannon about the place:

> Groups of individuals may [sic] form mutual protection associations: all will answer the call of any member for defence or for enforcement of his rights. In union there is strength. (p.12)

The practical inconvenience of this arrangement is that members are "on call" the entire time. The remedy for that travail is achieved (p.13) "in the usual manner by division of labour and exchange"; some people will become protection specialists and be paid for their work. The mutual protection associations now comprise subscribers and staff. For a variety of reasons (p.16), some mutual protection associations (MPAs) fare better than others and people, anxious to buy the best protection, will gravitate towards those which are strongest. In time, for this or that geographic locality, a dominant protective association will emerge. Summarising thus far, Nozick (pp.16-7) writes:

> Out of anarchy, pressed by spontaneous groupings, mutual-protection associations, division of labor, market pressures, economies of scale, and rational self-interest there arises something very much resembling a minimal state or a group of geographically distinct minimal states.

The essential character of these proto-states is their work as "night-watchmen" over the rights of their members. Beyond that they have no function; certainly they do not develop, fabricate or initiate policies for the distribution or redistribution of any goods. They are ultra-minimal states.

Nozick stresses that, though the invisible hand moves things, at the same time only those moves which are ethically required or permissible may be allowed. It follows that people's actions, though motivated in response to invisible hand pressures, must be at least morally permissible - and what is permissible is derivable from our primary natural rights. All individuals (p.102) may resist those systems or practices which, after due conscientious consideration, they find to be unfair or unreliable. We notice at once that, slight though this extension is on free market libertarian ethics, it is enough to free the B family from its ethical/practical paradox. If members of the B family decide A1 is being unfair towards them then they are entitled to resist. It also brings Nozick closer to the fold of familiar ethical reasoning. For instance, Nozick's position on this point runs parallel to Hobbes' escape clause. And, though it is a muted note in his argument, it is one which provides a link between the rights-based ethics of PI and the (often contrasted) deontological tradition. Nozick (pp.30-1) explicitly gives due to Kant on this point and, although this jumps forward a bit, it is worth highlighting here:

> Side constraints upon action reflect the underlying Kantian principle that individuals are ends and not merely means; they may not be sacrificed or used for the achieving of other ends without their consent.

But, to return to the character of rights and the workings of an invisible hand: the right to self-defence may be contracted out, say to the MPA so, when the MPA acts on behalf of a subscriber, it acts legitimately.[2] Similarly, when all those who subscribe to a protection agency do so to the same one, the resultant "dominant protective agency" (DPA) is still legitimate. At this stage, then, there is a *de facto* monopoly on the legitimate use of force and no individual's right to self-defence has been illicitly alienated; all members of the DPA and "independents" (people who are not subscribers to an MPA or the DPA) retain their right to take matters into their own hands - though, to be sure, that might be a "risky", "unreliable" thing to do.

That is the snag with this ultra-minimal state: within its circumstances some people have to contemplate seriously risky moves. Moves, that is, which are virtually foredoomed to failure and/or liable to cause unwarranted harm to others. Of particular concern to Nozick, here, is the plight of the independents. That is, those who, for whatever reasons (e.g. poverty or disinclination), are not members of the DPA but who live in the area controlled by it. These independents are practically powerless to enforce their rights when they confront DPA connections. The agency (p.109), by virtue of its strength, "alone is in the position to act soley by its own lights" - a palpable disadvantage to the independents. To cancel out this form of disadvantage (or risk), Nozick introduces the principle of compensation (which has been mentioned *en passant*, above), according to which (p.110), "in these circumstances those persons promulgating and benefiting from [a] prohibition must compensate those disadvantaged by it". In the present case, members of the DPA must compensate the independents in kind or money for the disadvantage their agency formation has created for them. This redistribution of goods is a further, necessary step towards the emergence of the minimal state.

For clarity, and to summarise, in Nozick's (pp.118-9) words:

> ... a Lockean state of nature will lead to single protective agencies dominant over geographical territories ... [W]ithout claiming to possess any rights uniquely, a protective agency dominant in a territory will occupy a unique position. Though each person has the right to act correctly to prohibit others from violating rights (...), only the dominant protective association will be able, without

41

sanction, to enforce correctness as it sees it. Its power makes it the arbiter of correctness; it determines what, for the purposes of punishment, counts as a breach of correctness. Our explanation does not assume or claim that might makes right. But might does make enforced prohibitions, even if no one thinks the mighty have a special entitlement to have realized in the world their own view of which prohibitions are correctly enforced.[3]

Anarchists, PI or otherwise, might well become restive at this point: might may not be right but what rights are left are insubstantial when confronted with the might of the DPA. Nozick (pp.130-1) anticipates nervous anarchists:

> Might not ... anarchists realize how individual efforts at hiring protection will lead ... to a state, and because they have historical evidence and theoretical grounds for the worry that the state is a Frankenstein monster that will run amuck and will not stay limited to minimal functions, might not they each prudently choose not to begin along that path?

He replies (p.131), this will not arrest the invisible hand process:

> It will be difficult for such concerted effort to succeed in blocking the formation of the state, since each individual will realize it is in his own individual interests to join a protective association (the more so as some others join), and his joining or not will not make the difference as to whether or not the state develops.

Given an earlier assurance that the state would not be justifiable if we were merely resigned to it this response has something bordering on contempt for the anarchist about it; is he not being told to resign himself to the inevitable? Quite possibly so, though no argumentative capital will be made out of that here. The damage would only be topical and, besides, Nozick could go on to say the anarchist must in any case be *compensated*, under procedural rights requirements, for whatever boundary crossings he is subject to in joining the proto-state.

But, it has been objected,[4] there is sufficient internal confusion in the argument to make it the case that the MS will not be able to evolve, that the invisible hand will not move with the implacable certainty Nozick supposes. The objection has implications which will be articulated presently. First, though, the objection itself.

The DPA and, later, the MS, it must not be forgotten, functions as a central, unified apparatus which makes decisions about boundary crossing procedures and prohibits others from doing so on the ground that that would "create a dangerous situation for all". How is this (safe) system to work? The answer is, under the aegis of a set of procedural rights (quite distinct from natural rights), exercised by the DPA/MS and which require no logically prior moral licence for them. "[I]t [DPA/MS] determines what ... counts as breach of correctness", i.e. what counts as "risky" undertaking of doubtful reliability, and remedies such breaches. The position is tricky: whilst accepting the fact that the DPA alone has effective power Nozick does not want to say that, by itself, legitimates its actions. If that is so, argues Paul (1982, p.74), the procedural rights will *have* to draw on some independent normative source. Then we should be able to have a roughly common working understanding as to the evaluative parameters of risky/not risky, reliable/unreliable behaviour. Yet, on Nozick's account, so far from that are we:

> ... there is no set of procedures common to all protection agencies that would enable public and independent verification of alleged procedural rights violations. (p.74)

Moreover, everybody retains the right to unilateral normative decisions. Practically speaking, acting unilaterally might well be risky but that does gainsay the entitlement. And the entitlement licences any agent to question the procedural rights of any DPA. Paul (p.74) says,

> ... so long as there is a plurality of views about what constitutes procedural justice, it is morally impermissible to move from anarchy to statism. [The result is] stalemated anarchy.

Here it is not intended to join Paul in taking this to be a crippling blow to Nozick's argument for the MS. Only in a formal sense is there a stalemate for, presumably, a DPA whose procedures are challenged by, say, an independent might well concede the right to challenge and yet

43

proceed with its intentions unaltered; this might outrage the independent who, analogously to the peons finds his rights are insubstantial, but it is no stalemate. However, Paul does draw attention to a certain degree of internal messiness with Nozick's position. *Prima facie*, Nozick says once the state of nature decays into feuding (a) the state is legitimated and (b) will arise out of the decomposition of anarchy. (b) begins as an economic process which, in order to avoid such phenomena as the peon relationship, requires the introduction of moral side-constraints, including procedural rights. But here is the strength of Paul's point: if they are simply a matter for decision by whoever runs the operations of the DPA, procedures might be variously scant, eccentric or self-interested to a provocative degree; rather than being a brake on contention, they might just as well propel it. In which case, evidently, the tables turn on Nozick's reply to the anarchists: the self-interested concern to reduce risks might be as much grounds for *leaving* the DPA as for joining. Being dominant is not an inviolable position ... as many once-hegemonic organisations have learned to their cost.

Thus, the point of transition from the nightwatchman state to the minimal state, where Nozick recommends the side constraint of requiring members of the association to pay it to meet the costs of compensating - in kind or cash - independents, is crucial. He is perfectly correct: an agency which claims the right to exact funds from its members to finance the provision of public goods to anybody in its territory is recognisably a state. That is not at issue. What is, is the belief that this state is necessary to halt, and reverse, the inevitable slide from anarchy into self-defeating anarchy. The matter can be debated on two fronts. Firstly, possessive individualists, people such as Nozick takes them to be, could very well make a mess of things over procedural rights: they might congregate for protection then dispute the method (and maybe the price) of it, defect, get into trouble as independents, congregate again, disagree...not stalemate but certainly unproductive. Secondly, we might inquire if the benefits of the MS can be achieved outside it and in, say, an acephalous society. If that can be achieved then something else will have occurred: a possible path will have been mapped out *between* the highly volatile libertarian anarchy discussed in chapter 2 and the supposed need for a state to stabilise that volatility.

The requirements of Nozickian PIs, it might be worth reminding ourselves are: (i) recognition of their natural rights, (ii) compensation for boundary crossings into them and (iii) procedural rights to regulate (ii) processes. Before the attempt is made to indicate how these could be accommodated in an acephalous community, a word of explanation about the chosen model might be wise.

On the one hand, out of the two million-odd years of human existence the species has lived in acephalous societies for most of them. Thus even the great ancient empires, the Aztecs, Egyptians, Babylonians and Chinese, though active five thousand years and more ago, are but a minute dot on a time-line 2 million years long. And as for modern states, nine hundred years old at the outside, they have microbe dimensions at the very end of the time-line. Though it might be regarded as eccentric, it is still possible (in terms of longevity) to regard anarchy as normal and archy as delinquent. On the other hand, for all that the modern state is a *parvenu*, it is now ubiquitous and betrays no signs of falling out of vogue. Quite the contrary, when this or that state collapses - which happens quite often - it is replaced by another(s) almost at once. Some small, and fast disappearing,[5] tribal communities aside, the only contemporary evidence to be had of anarchy is of the self-defeating kind. The state, as the typical mode of socio-political control, is here to stay. It is hard to imagine how, now or in the future, things could be otherwise. Guided by such a perception as this, it might be thought that when, in a moment, an example from the ancient world is brought forward to contend with modern archy the challenge is surely precious romanticism. Two points will be made in reply. Firstly, the immediate use of the example is limited to illustrating how something equivalent to Nozick's state of nature contains procedures which make his account of the need to invent the state redundant. That is a limited, though legitimate, philosophical task. Secondly, from the seed of the ancient world example, this book will attempt the germination of an anarchy which could not only survive but regulate the social, economic and political forces of the modern world.

To turn now to the first challenge - that of safeguarding rights to personal security and private property, compensation for boundary-crossings by safe, reliable procedures and without the need for a state doing this or defraying the costs through compulsory acquisition of funds from members. Joseph R. Peden (1971) gives a description of the politico-legal system of Celtic Ireland in his "Stateless Societies: Ancient Ireland". The contention that follows depends on having an outline description of some salient features of that society to hand.

Celtic, or Ancient Ireland comprised a loose-knit grouping of polities, called *tuatha* (singular: *tuath*)[6] for well over a thousand years - until its conquest by England was all but complete, in fact. Pagan to begin with, these acephalous communities became Christian without that event altering the structure of their society. They did not develop a theocracy or some other cephalous administration, for instance. For as far back as there is record there is evidence of intercourse with centralised, petty states such as the Norman and Scandinavian chieftainships. Again, these relationships did not undermine the *tuath* system. Perhaps the saddest, and bravest, testimony to the resilience of the Ancient Irish way of life is that it did not collapse until after *five hundred years* of continual attack from England - crown and commonwealth alike.

The membership of a *tuath* comprised all propertied men, members of the professions and skilled artisans. The sum of the landed property held by members was its territorial extent. Membership of a *tuath* was an alienable and voluntary matter. There were no binding obligations, customary or legal, to any particular *tuath*. People moved from one to another according to convenience.

The *tuath* members met annually to discuss matters of common concern and to decide on collective action when this seemed necessary. The *tuath* also elected a king at the annual assembly. The kings were not sovereigns, they were cult/religious personages. They were elected from a particular family though there was no prescribed lineal descent. Sometimes, even, there were two nominees...in which case two kings were elected. The kings, I repeat, had no legislative or coercive authority. When their supervision of religious events displeased they could be, and were, deposed without this occasioning untoward social discord or political hiatus. There was no presumption or practice of sovereignty. There was no specialised legislature, no police, no central revenue or redistributive systems. So far as inter-*tuath* politics goes, when they became heated they sometimes formed temporary confederations and fought others. By familiar standards, war was little more than a short-lived brawl fought on very amateurish lines for that was all prudence and limited resources allowed. Some *tuatha* were comparatively large, others smaller but, unlike Nozick's MPAs, none grew to dominate the others, none achieved hegemony. Peden (p.4) says that because they had no taxes none could afford the effort of establishing itself as the strongest, dominant *tuath* - even if it had wanted to.

Law was customary in Ancient Ireland and, common to *all tuatha*, was handed down from one generation to the next. However, this was not an inflexible inheritance; it adapted to altered needs. Legal procedures, including glosses on extant law to cope with emergent contingencies, and the processing of actions were the responsibility of schooled, professional jurists, called *filid*. *Filid* were somewhat like modern arbitrators in that they did just that - arbitrate. There being no state which might otherwise have retained or licensed them, they always acted in a private capacity. Law itself and all actions before it were "civil". *Filid* were chosen to hear cases on the basis of their skill and reputation in law. If there was a quarrel between two parties in the same *tuath* then their seconds, so to speak, would have to make the arrangements for a particular arbitrator to hear the matter. If, on the other hand, there was contention between people from different *tuatha* or one disputant hurriedly departed his *tuath*, hearing and judgement could still be effected because the *filid*, in their professional capacity, moved and acted freely in any *tuath*, quite independently of any particular *tuath* membership they might have had. At no stage was the process of law inhibited by parochial differences - there were none in this particular regard. Moreover, though it might seem odd to us, not to say incredible, *filid* law was not backed-up by some form of police. Matters are very different now; even our civil law is reinforced with bailiffs and police. Understandably the question can be asked: how were *filid* rulings executed?

By way of reply, the first thing to note is that penalties in Ancient Ireland did not include corporal, penal or capital inflictions. Thus arrest, incarceration and execution were not issues with which a defendant had to reckon. However, all members of a *tuath* were linked - usually through kinship lines - to a system of fiscal sureties. Peden (p.4) summarises what must have been a comprehensive set of inter-obligations:

Men were linked together by a number of individual relationships by which they were obligated to stand surety for one another guaranteeing that wrongs would be righted, debts paid, judgements

47

honored, and the law enforced ... Almost every conceivable legal transaction was worked out through the taking and giving of sureties.

Such a system met the test of practicability insofar as people consented to be bound by it.[7] But what of free riders? The law itself supplied the answer for the code declared, "He who disregards all things is paid by neither God nor man". In effect those who went in contempt of the law found themselves ostracised not only from their own *tuath* but from all of them. To be sure, had circumstances been such that communities were widely dispersed and communication between them poor to non-existent, the threat of ostracism would not be very discouraging; the rogue could simply set up somewhere else where his character and deeds were, so far, unknown. But in this case the *tuatha* are immediate neighbours and communication across the entire country very active and effective. Thus ostracism was a potent threat for its victims were, literally, on their own and faced ruin. The stakes would have to be desperate indeed for that to be considered a serious option.

Celtic Ireland was a state of nature, in Nozick's terms. There was no centralised, specialist rights enforcement agency; no MPAs, let alone DPAs or MS. Furthermore, there was no system of compulsory acquisition of goods to meet the costs of compensation for independents and the like. Why, then, did the whole thing not decompose into feuding, into self-defeating anarchy? Of course it would not have had the people been angelically disposed - but the evidence suggests not all of them were. On the contrary there were mechanisms for dealing with far from angelic characters and it is fatuous to suppose they had those mechanisms to no purpose. Indeed, the people could have had very PI perspectives and desires. So, again, why did this system not go the same way as Nozick's most favoured anarchy? The answer to that question promises to be significant: it might even expose the fact that PIs are not moved into statism because (willy nilly) the state of nature is constitutionally degenerative.

The *tuatha* had two things which Nozick would agree are necessary to control boundary-crossing and manage pay-outs when they occur. To use his terms, they had a firm way (the law) to settle each dispute which was operated through a central, unified apparatus (the *filid*). What they did not have were specialists in the use of force (commissioned to protect subscribers' rights) and compulsory appropriation (to pay for security -

let us simply call this tax from now on). At the same time the *tuatha/filid* system does seem to answer Nozick's requirements of the MS, viz. (a) natural rights are, or can be, protected (b) but when their boundaries are crossed there is a system of compensation and (c) there are reliable, safe procedures for ensuring that (b) is carried through. For PIs (amongst others), it seems the necessary conditions for preventing the state of nature collapsing into self-defeating anarchy are (a), (b) and (c) which can be provided for without specialist enforcement agencies and taxes. That is because the socio-legal system combined with the practice of diffuse sanctions makes it contrary to short- or long-term self-interest to free ride. Moreover, we might add, the Kantian element Nozick adds to PIsm promises to make the work of the legal system that much easier. The answer to the question above follows almost trivially: although the state of nature *could* decompose under certain circumstances[8] it is not congenitally disposed to. Certain implications are now apparent. If the MS was inescapable it could not be derived from a most favoured anarchy. If the MS is not inescapable it is an option (alongside the state of nature). On economic grounds alone (quite apart from it constraining less the exercise of rights) the state of nature is preferable. Nozick was quoted at the beginning of this chapter as saying, quite rightly, that "we ... must consider what arrangements might be made within a state of nature to deal with the inconveniences" of boundary-crossings. That process of consideration has been started in this chapter and, it is hoped, achieved a measure of success in showing that anarchic doubt about the necessity of states does reveal acephalous practical political possibilities. The concomitant to that claim is that though, as Dunn says (1990, p.1), "Defining the mutual rights and duties of states and their individual human subjects has been a central preoccupation of modern politics for several centuries and may perhaps be said to define the historical terrain of modern politics itself," yet leaving things at that is methodologically incomplete. That is a modest enough claim. But it opens the way for a more ambitious one: anarchy is not just a theoretical stance from which to charge cephalous systems to improve their moral condition; it can be sustained as a genuine political option. Some modest steps in the direction of achieving that ambition are taken in chapters 5-7 to follow.

Retrospectively, consideration of the *tuatha* system has achieved another advantage. There is little doubt that a Rothbardian libertarianism is so delicately poised on the edge that very little is required to upset it into degenerative anarchy. To illustrate that was a major purpose of the last chapter. The minimal state would be a means of pulling free-market economics, with its attendant dangers of boundary-crossings, back from the edge; that has not been doubted. It has been challenged, however, that the MS is a practical necessity. The *tuatha* successfully pick out a pathway which makes the MS unnecessary.

So, some of the supposed difficulties about being possessive individualists in a state of nature have been met. But where does that leave invisible hand explanation? Could it be that it is no more than a methodological fantasy? On the face of it that seems too severe an inference. That brings us back to the first question. Briefly, in the following chapter, I propose to answer that question for, even though its methodological efficacy has been questioned here, we might still have use for it, albeit in restricted form. And, in the process of answering the question, I shall draw out some comparisons between the PI arguments treated so far. These, in turn, will be used to help pick the way forward towards practical anarchy.

Notes

1   In the interests of brevity and trading upon the wide-spread familiarity with Nozick's methodology this will not be described here. However, Nozick gives an account of invisible hand explanation in *Anarchy, State & Utopia,* pp.18-22. In so far as it bears on the very possibility of sustainable anarchy it will be reviewed in chapter 4, below.

2   I leave to one side for the moment the possible objection that the putative inference begs a question about exactly what sorts of acts the MPA is going to claim legitimacy for under this scheme.

3   For an historical instance where there was a transfer from a state of nature to something very like a DPA see Anderson, T.L. & Hill, P.J. (1979), "An American Experiment in Anarcho-Capitalism: the Not So Wild, Wild West", *Journal of Libertarian Studies,* pp.9-29.

4   By Paul, J. "The Withering of Nozick's Minimal State", in Paul, J. (ed), *Reading Nozick,* Oxford: Blackwell, 1982, pp.68-76.

5   Murdoch, G.P. (1968), "The Current Status of the World's Hunting & Gathering Peoples" in Lee, R.B. & DeVore, I. (eds), *Man the Hunter,* Aldine: Chicago, pp.13-20.

6   When referring to the historical cases I shall italicise the words and when using them to refer to the philosophical model being pieced together here they will be written in plain script.

7   A remark not as trivial as it might sound. *Not* resisting arrest to the nth of one's ability, *not* spending every moment in gaol trying to escape it, *walking* to the gallows are all forms of (albeit parsimonious) consent to what is being imposed on one.

8   For a case-history of something startlingly similar to Nozick's hypothetical see Turnbull, C.M. (1973), *The Mountain People,* London: Jonathan Cape, and ch.4, below.

4 Intermission

This is not a chapter in the fully grown sense. Yet it contains reflections on the story so far which have argumentative bearing on the story to come; conceptually it ushers in the constructive material forthcoming from the critical material just gone. For that reason it warrants separation into a section on its own; it is simply a matter of convenience to call it a chapter. It is, however, very much an intermission. It is a pause between the first part where the *dramatis personae*, to keep the metaphor going, have turned away from one pathway to anarchism without finding it necessary, therefore, to take to archy. On the contrary, they have hit upon the idea of another possible anarchic way. When the curtain goes up in chapter 5, the action centres on what can profitably be pioneered in that way.

So far three perspectives on anarchy, all of which have a preoccupation with the centrality of possessive individualism as a politico-economic motive, have been explored. To various extents each direction taken has been guided by an invisible hand explanation (IH). This is explicitly so in Nozick, tacit with Hobbes and Rothbard. It is quite possible to agree with Nozick that there is a "certain lovely quality" in invisible hand explanations - that they highlight how a sequence of events leads to a result which nobody intended but which, however, has every appearance of design. Something else attractive about them might be how they move between two explanatory extremes. On the one hand full-blooded intentional agency accounts which, at the fringe if not beyond, suppose the sufficient conditions for events in (large scale, multi-faceted) human enterprises are intentions. This belief overlooks the frequency with which events, or enterprises, turn out at variance with the intentions of all concerned and, perhaps, sometimes in spite of them. To take the burning building case of entropic anarchy, it is everybody's intention to leave the building uninjured and everybody acts single-mindedly on that intention but because they act unilaterally, jamming up the exit, a distressingly large number of people are injured or killed. The other extreme is occupied by a variety of determinist explanatory views, e.g. physical determinism and structural determinism.[1] The latter, for our purposes, is a counter-weight to full-blooded intentionality. It maintains that socio-political events are shaped by, and sufficiently explained in terms of, structural matrices and their dynamics alone. But it is surely implausible to say of events, even very large ones like revolutions, that how they came about has nothing to do with intentions.[2] Here, again, IH explanation is felicitous: people's intentional actions *do* contribute to the nature of events even though actual outcomes are not always - seldom? - anticipated.

It might be that a considerable amount of social and political philosophy draws on IH explanation, explicitly or otherwise. A case can be made out for Hobbes' drawing on it, in a rough and ready kind of way, e.g. where the possibility of anarchy is indicated by him. Hobbesians have two political options open to them. Firstly, they can rid themselves of the problems which arise out of state of nature n-person, non-cooperative "games" (or self-defeating anarchy) by contracting to institute a sovereign to enforce co-operation. This is an intentional agenda (at time T1) based on rational situation and self analyses and committed to certain outcomes. Thus there is nothing hidden about the hand which impels matters to the institution of sovereignty, the forfeit of the right to self-government and the establishment of peace. However, if the sovereign then behaves contrary to the remaining rights-interests of the subjects (those to life, liberty and access to the means to a "commodious life") the affected subjects may use the escape clause, viz., by whatever means at their disposal, including those of "warre", to resist (at time T2). This is not because they want to; it is quite the contrary to their intended political scheme - so was the behaviour of their sovereign. This is IH at least to the extent that a pattern is forming, out of the actions of the agents, which was not intended (or desired). The process continues: pushed out of the state, as it were, agents now have to *do* *something* with the state of nature (provided their level of pessimism has not sunk to nihilist depths). Perhaps stimulated by the sheer discomfort of their circumstances, people might "discover" Hobbes' reply to the Foole, that it is rational to co-operate voluntarily in the state of nature.[3] And, it follows then, the state of nature is not necessarily self-defeating anarchy. That implies that the benefits of society (of a sort) are obtainable anarchically. Achieving anarchy by this means can be understood in IH terms. Intentional actions, and other circumstances, from -T1 until T2 explain how comes it the escape clause is used, for all that its use was not foreseen at T1. Similarly at T2+ an IH partly accounts for the development of a practicable state of nature, i.e. keeping the peace by maximising voluntary co-operation in iterated, multi-partnered PD. Hobbes, I repeat, is not an exclusive IH theorist but, thus far, a place has been found for IH explanation in the evolution of his PIs from a degenerative archy to sustainable anarchy. In other words, IH is one aspect of the mutation.

Crusoe economics, however, seem to be a much more clear cut case, almost a paradigm, of IH explanation. Crusoe's early actions are motivated by certain corporeal needs. In meeting those needs, adapting to pressures of circumstance and refining his survival skills to the point where he and others can enjoy the proceeds of production surplus, it is as if the resulting economic pattern was the product of a design but, in fact, there was no such design "in mind" at the outset or during the process. Though, on reflexion and subsequently, its proponents carve from the experience the libertarian creed, the "praxeology" is not intentional. At the same time, as I have attempted to illustrate in chapter 2, there is a darker side to the movements of this hand and pure liberty, by itself, turns out to be a somewhat chilling prospectus for anarchy. Firstly, in the peon-relationship, A1 could successfully argue (if he chose) before arbitration that he has no case to answer with regard to his treatment of the peons and, though the latter have no defence under the creed, yet they have no practical option but to violate A1's rights. Secondly, the creed does not have the normative capacity to enable it to resolve certain classes of disputed rights entitlements, such as those of the Indians and the homesteader. Market driven anarchy, without what Nozick calls moral side-constraints, is ethically and politically too unstable a configuration to contain and control the volatile confrontations it can catalyse. It is as if libertarian argument is led by an invisible hand but it (the argument) fails to anticipate where, having got this far, it will be led next.

Moreover, the "pure freedom" perspective lacks that very human feature of other-regardingness which is almost a psychological intuition. In chapter 3 it was noted that Nozick gives the intuition Kantian normative explicitness (nobody is to be treated as - merely - a means) and then assumes an anarchy where most people respect it. Thus, libertarian like Rothbard though he is, he *adds* a normative dimension to the state of nature. The challenge which he then sets up is: a state would be justified only if it be superior to this, most favourable, anarchy. The results of the challenge - so far as Nozick is concerned - turn out to be far less equivocal than those provided by Hobbes. Working with PI material Nozick concludes that the MS *must* be invented. In fact, though it might have appeared otherwise at the outset, anarchy has no more political substance to it than a hypothetical function in the IH explanation as to why the MS occurs and is justified. *Any* moral delinquency in the state of nature is sufficient to cause it to degenerate into self-defeating anarchy and that, in turn, will begin the invisible hand moves to MPAs, DPAs and, finally, MSs (inclusive of procedural side-constraints).

Now, though the arguments of Hobbes and Rothbard have symptomatic features of IH explanations it would be too much to say that because of their IH aspects their arguments are, in some respect or another, wrong - or right for that matter. To put the point another way: the relationship between IH explanation and their political theories is coincidental and I can see no necessary reason why, if there is anything awry with the manifestation of the former in their arguments, there are epistemological consequences for the latter. Things might be rather different for Nozick, however. For a start, he espouses IH methodology with ebullience though that, by itself, need not be of philosophical consequence. But, secondly, what is *really* going on when the invisible hand promotes an end which was not part of anybody's intention? Does it mean that the hand moves a bit like a determinist causal process so that, once in train, the outcome is inevitable (for all that we could not predict the outcome)? In which case, the IH explanation of the minimal state is epistemologically strong and, by implication, the *tuatha* of chapter 3 are relegated to the shadowy world of counter-factuals, possible merely in the sense of being non-self contradictions. Nozick (1974, pp.8-22), in talking about IH explanations, makes no explicit statement to that effect. What he does say is this:

The specially satisfying quality of invisible-hand explanations (a quality I hope is possessed by this book's account of the state) is partially explained by its connection with the notion of fundamental explanation ... Fundamental explanations of a realm are explanations of the realm in other terms ... (pp.18-9)

IHs avoid circularity, which is all to the good. But if that is all there is to it why celebrate non-circular political argument as invisible hand? Why not just remind people that the product is not contained in the process? Besides, doing this is not a very singular achievement; Hobbes and Rothbard have both managed and Rousseau, amongst others, will manage likewise, as we shall see in chapter 5.

Perhaps - and this is pure conjecture, since there is nothing to go on from Nozick himself - IH explanations, containing as they do both intentional and circumstantial ingredients, show how, once a social matrix (amongst others) becomes dynamic, it will in all likelihood move in *that* direction, rather than any other. This has the argumentative convenience which was pointed out above: it traces a path between the infelicities of full-blooded intentionality explanations and (mere) structural determinism. So, for the sake of argument, let us go along with it for a moment. It is at least consistent with Nozick's claim that if the emergence of the MS can be explained *and* that explanation has involved no morally impermissible moves, then the MS is justified.

The question then is: how compelling are IH explanations? By this I mean, how much does the IH part contribute to the credibility at least, if not exclusiveness, of the overall account being essayed? In the next few paragraphs these questions will be explored. The ulterior reason for doing that is to begin to raise the status, as it were, of the *tuatha* from theoretically just possible option to robustly plausible option. The enterprise is begun here (a) because it helps to present IH explanations in what are, arguably, their true colours which are less attractive, epistemologically, than a strong interpretation of Nozick seems to suggest and (b) to further consolidate the foundation on which to build a pathway to anarchy.

Within *tuatha*, Nozickian PIs could live without the need for coercing people into a level of co-operation necessary to maximise the average benefits from public goods. Here, however, we should proceed with some caution for the modal "could" might be taken to betray some argumentative weakness; a *sotto voce* admission that this is a very long

56

shot. Suppose, for example, the proposition that PIs *could* (theoretically) live acephalously is confronted by an epistemically vigorous invisible hand counter-claim that, once we take into account certain PI motive forces, the MS must, on very high probability, be invented? The power of that counter-claim will now be challenged by showing that, in order to get the invisible hand going in the direction Nozick thinks it will (or any other, for that matter), there must be something else, besides the hand, at work (this is the weaker interpretation of IH). Otherwise the two million years of living disproof (including Ancient Ireland) of Nozick's rejection of anarchy must itself be rejected ... and that is altogether too far-fetched.

As a subordinate point to the main issue in chapter 4 some outline of IH explanation was interleaved where called for. However, for the purposes of this chapter the account of it needs to be unified. Broadly, an IH explanation shows

> ... how some overall pattern or design, which one would have thought had to be produced by an individual's or group's successful attempt to realize the pattern, instead was produced and maintained by a process that in no way had the overall pattern or design "in mind." (p.18)

People's various responses to force of circumstance bring about some new pattern which nobody had intended. In the present case, through a series of responses to state of nature conditions, Nozick's PIs have arrived at the MS "which claims a monopoly on force while protecting all", as Wolff (1991) puts it. Bearing in mind that, in the process of constructing the MS, as it were, people may only do things which are morally required or permissible, Nozick has two prongs to his argument: (1) at least the MS is justified and (2) at most it is justified. It is with regard to (1) that Nozick's argumentative method is of interest here for, as we have seen, he contends that by an IH process (with no impermissible moves made), he has achieved a state polity superior to the best anarchic alternative; the MS, it follows, is legitimate. If that is so then one strong version of the anarchists' claims is refuted. This strong claim is that no state is legitimate. There is no interest in defending the strong claim here. On the contrary, it would be manifest folly, for instance, to stand by self-defeating anarchy rather than be tainted with any statehood on the grounds that no state is legitimate.

The present position is this: what Nozick claims to be the most favoured acephalous condition is, *a fortiori*, self-defeating anarchy. It has to be to get the IH to move his way at all ... and, as a response to the degenerative state of nature, the MS is legitimate. But, we can counter, the state of nature does not have to be as Nozick supposes - and has frequently not been. This provides us with a warrant to question the epistemological standing of IH explanation and can be investigated further.

First, though, I shall outline a case history which is living proof, in a sense, of Nozick's hypothetical degenerative state of nature. Then, still using the example, I will try to pin-point the intrinsic limitations of IH explanations - to the extent that, by themselves, they explain very little in an epistemologically strong way though they might well help us see, in retrospect, how things turned out as they did.

In the far north-east of Uganda, live (lived?) a people called the Ik.[4] They are peaceful, acephalous hunter-gatherers, who, in addition, carry on some poor agriculture on the steep slopes of their mountain country. They live in the middle of a cluster of warrior pastoralists: the Turkana, Karimojong, Dodoth (a.k.a. Dodos) and Didinga. These pastoralists give a lot of time to raiding each other's cattle and the Ik, who are non-belligerents in this scheme of things, trade in intelligence. They collect and sell information to the warring tribes, about each other's tactical movements, for which they are paid in tobacco, blankets and other goods they would have difficulty procuring otherwise. So far the Ik are a viable community, internally cohesive and symbiotically related to their neighbours. Then, in the mid nineteen-sixties, a national park was gazetted in the valley (the Kidepo Valley) below their mountain. Where hunting and gathering in the valley had been the Ik's principal source of meat and edible plants, this was now denied them. During the consequent shortage of food, members of the community took to keeping what little they could find and not sharing (a breakdown in reciprocity - see chapter 6), stealing from each other, letting their elderly and sick die unattended - even killing them if they had some food about or other negotiable goods. The fabric of community was torn up. It became a stark case of every man, woman and child for themselves; live and let die. Something, perhaps, of the life of those unalloyed egoists which Hobbes glimpsed in his imagined state of nature is reflected in the reality of life among the Ik. Turnbull writes (1973, p.290):

58

Such interaction as there is within this system is one of mutual exploitation. That is the relationship between all, old, young, parent and child, brother and sister, husband and wife, friend and friend. That is how it already is with the Ik. They are brought together by self-interest alone, and the system takes care that such association is of a temporary nature and cannot flourish into anything as dysfunctional as affection or trust.

The case is living (if that is the right word) proof of Nozick's degenerative state of nature. Moreover, it is an instance of a (negative) invisible hand occurrence. I take it that no Ik intended and only the prescient foresaw the destruction of their way of life. Nevertheless, when all sought to preserve themselves from starvation they did destroy the tribe and, possibly, by non-cooperation, accelerated the process of starvation. Taking the tough-minded anarchic line and dismissing invisible hand explanations of, e.g. the degeneration of state of nature communities as mere hypotheticals, as part of a strategy to discredit Nozick's line of argument, will not do. Such events occur.

But now something becomes very obvious, if it was not already. The invisible hand is a *metaphor*. When Y occurred it was as *if* antecedent events X1...Xn were under the direction of an invisible hand. Psychologically the figure of speech might very well be an aid to comprehension. "How on earth did this new social configuration come about? Surely somebody must have figured it out?". "Not so ... it was an invisible hand occurrence. You see ...". But the *real* explanation of how Y came about makes essential reference to X1...Xn, not to IH. And something else is now equally clear: Ik society collapsed because the people were starving and they were starving because they were excluded from their main source of food and that was because, etc ... but, of course, things could have turned out otherwise. For example, the Ik could have become proficient poachers or left Morenyang (their mountain) or UNICEF might have come with famine relief. As to what actually transpired was to be explained, in part, by a number of contingencies specific to the case. All that reference to an invisible hand would do would be to remind us that nobody intended that the Kidepo Valley National Park should have the effect it did on the Ik. Likewise, if we return to Nozick's state of nature, we readily understand that the IH explains, or emphasises, that nobody intended or planned the MS. But to the positive side of the explanation the IH adds very little, if anything. That task is accomplished by the claim that people will feud in the state of nature so they will form MPAs and so by degrees the MS comes into being. Equally possible, depending on contingencies which might well include agents' intentions, is for the tuath to stabilise Nozick's state of nature. All this, of course, does not weaken Nozick's argument (1) that the MS can at least be justified - it surely is if the alternative is self-defeating anarchy. But (2) does not fare so well: the MS is not now the only polity which is justifiable.

It might be that IH explanation is bewitching; that it is as if, seeing it move in one direction, one believes that *is* its direction, forgetting that it could move in many others. In actual fact, it can even back-hand. Suppose the transition from the ultra-minimal to the minimal state is all but complete when two non-Nozick events take place. Firstly, the independents refuse to be prohibited from settling their own scores and, secondly, members of the ultra-minimal state refuse to pay for the protection of non-members, such as the independents. If the neoteric state is going to survive, surely it must needs take these deviants in hand and have the prohibition and levy enforced. *Prima facie* the act of enforcement might be an illicit boundary-crossing but that is not the immediate concern. What is, is that the independents and those who refuse to pay the levy can, when threatened by the MS, use Hobbes' escape clause. They could argue that when they are threatened by the state it has degenerated from its role in defence of rights to that of rights invader - and they are morally entitled to resist. In support of Nozick, it might be interjected here that resistance to the MS - use of the escape clause - is impermissible because it is risky and unreliable. However, though this might be true sometimes, it is a very circumstantial point. For instance, the level of risk and unreliability in levy refusal depends partly on the number of people who do refuse. One gets to a point where refusal to pay the levy is no risk at all; as Nozick himself said, there is strength in numbers. When one uses the escape clause, this is a two stage venture: not only should one calculate the chances of successfully resisting or otherwise evading state coercion but one should also reckon with the level of risks and reliability attendant upon reverting to the state of nature. On this point Nozick's reasoning is very similar to that of the "standard" reading of Hobbes: it is foolhardy to jump from the frying pan into the fire. And the reasoning is prudentially sound. Assuming, for the sake of argument, the wits of those contemplating the escape clause are not hopelessly befuddled by some passion, reason will inhibit their inclination to depart the state if the state of nature is going to be P-inferior to it. Here, however, the argument of chapter 3 has a wrap-around effect: it is not P-inferior if one models the state of nature on the *tuatha*, or something sufficiently like them as to keep the peace and maximise the PI pay-offs through voluntary co-operation. In that case the escape clause is a rational political option for possessive individualists[5] who are confronted by a situation which calls for some action on their part. On this account, then, the better interpretation of invisible hand explanations is the weaker one. They are indeed pedagogic devices which aid one's comprehension of historical events. Their function in retrospective explanations is quite clear: given certain circumstances one can see how events turned out as they did (without anybody specifically intending those outcomes). They do not contain epistemologically vigorous elements of determination and prediction of events. And, albeit without deliberately setting out to use a Nozickian IH model of explanation, how one explains the evolution of the *tuath* itself turns out to be an invisible hand explanation of a sort. In so far as the tuath argument develops out of strategies for coping with more immediate circumstances it parallels Nozick's form of explanation though it is less urgently insistent that this is practically the only way the hand could have moved. On that point, against the pre-emptive force of the hand to move events so much more one way than another, rests the argument against Nozick. The consequences are these: the MS is justifiable as a response to a degenerative state of nature *but* it is not the only justifiable polity; on the contrary, if tuath anarchy pre-empts the degenerative state of nature the MS becomes a political redundancy.

To end this intermission one can note that a protocol amongst the PI arguments considered here is emerging with regard to the escape clause (the clause which legitimates anarchy, as it were). Most strongly for it is Rothbard, most strongly against it is Nozick. Some of my effort so far has been given to outlining where these strenuously unequivocal positions in regard to the escape clause do not of themselves sweep all argument before them. In between the two modern writers is Hobbes who, so early in the development of modern political thought, saw options: a case for the state and another for the state of nature. Admittedly he did not inquire further into anarchy other than to say acephalous confederations were possible. But, riding on that train of thought here, it has been shown how the *tuath* system could meet the moral requirements of PIs without the invisible hand having to lift a finger in the direction of archy.

Finally, one cannot say for certain but it seems very likely that the historical *tuatha* did not have a self-consciously worked out PI ideal of the good life such as Rothbard and Nozick have. The question should be asked, then: could PIs live in the political world of the *tuath*? In the next chapter an attempt will be made to answer that question. And from that attempt will emerge the outline shape of anarchic community. Not, I hasten to add, because there is a teleological commitment to locate practical anarchy in community but because viable anarchy requires it.

Notes

1   See Skocpol T. (1979), *States & Social Revolutions*, Cambridge: Cambridge University Press. Skocpol explains the French, Russian and Chinese revolutions with a "nonvoluntarist, structural" methodology which claims that the "sufficient distinctive causes" of these revolutions are to be found in the international and national political relations and in the intra-state social and economic relations. With these structural causes to hand the "basic transformations of a society's state and class structures" are explained (p.154 and *passim*).

2   This does not mean that intending to x is any guarantee that x will occur. All that is implied is: if A, having intended it, x's then part of the explanation of why x occurred is that A intended it.

3   It has to be discovered at this stage rather than, say, at -T1, because otherwise the act of institution is otiose.

4   My knowledge of these people is first-hand but the data here is corroborated in Turnbull, C.M. (1973), *The Mountain People*, London: Jonathan Cape.

5   I stress its viability for PIs because, by contrast to those who are dispositionally or morally more communitarian, they are the harder group to convince of the benefits of co-operation. The latter group is inclined to co-operate in any case - and there is no point in arguing with the converted.

5 Authority, individuals & stateless political community

People, large numbers of them in fact, have gone their way firm in their belief that being involved in government and policy decisions was (is) *not* their place. And critics of polities where government is an exclusive specialism and obedience to it expected as of right might think of such as slave states (or little better).[1] The critical reaction is usually premissed on one or both of two positions: (a) an emotive and personal dislike for being subject to the will of others and/or (b) a moral claim for (some measure of) individual autonomy in normative action - which can be construed as either a right or a duty. I take it that people who have no belief in, nor could be encouraged to show any interest in (a) and/or (b) would see nothing particularly attractive about anarchy. Even democratic archy, for that matter, can be expected to hold little appeal for such people whether they be rulers or ruled. Obvious this might be but worth being quite clear about before the politics of anarchy are attended to any further for the appeal of anarchy is substantially founded on the *presumed* value of these individualist traits. So much so that, in respect of (a) and/or (b) anarchism is, in spirit, flatly uncompromising:

[anarchism is] the negation of the principle of Authority in social organisations and the hatred of all constraints that originate in institutions founded on that principle. (Faure, 1986, p.62)

Perhaps so but the "negation of the principle of Authority" is consistent with self-defeating anarchy. The burning building example is ample illustration. Political authority is (sometimes) a system, which comes in a variety of forms, for co-ordinating the activities of humans in society where, without co-ordination, the results are P-inferior. To be sure, what is assumed under the mantle of political authority sometimes exceeds that role and, at others, neglects it. In the history of anarchic thought, many anarchists have become so as a result of witnessing excessive or neglectful statist polities. Nevertheless, it is a mistake to reject political authority and its social regulative functions as if nothing but harm can come of them. The situation is quite the reverse: without political authority, self-defeating anarchy - by definition harmful - is immanent. If anarchy is to be practicable, a viable choice alongside other polities, in the arena of political philosophy it must at least address the matter of authority (understood as a means of P-optimising pay-offs, if nothing else).

Of course the case for saying political authority is required is contingent. Anarchists could be so homogenously composed that the question of how they arrange themselves politically is redundant. They might be intellectual, emotional and physical clones, for instance. Or they could be ethically so much in concert, one with another, that resolving normative differences is otiose. *A propos*, it was Aquinas, I think - though sadly I cannot now trace the reference - who remarked that only angels could be anarchists. But for us the blunt fact of the matter is we are neither material clones nor angelic. We fall short on both accounts. So the problem of what kind of political arrangements (authority) will suit remains - contingently, yes, but still importantly. As far as anarchy is concerned, for example, there might be a difficulty here in as much as individualists (hailed by anarchists from Godwin to the present as the *sine qua non* of humanity) will be inclined to answer their own wills rather than anybody else's. Yet there will be circumstances when the rational means to their ends require co-operation with others who have a like regard for their own wills. That is, they will have to (voluntarily) co-operate if, on the one side, they choose not to live solitary, mole-like lives and if, on the other, they are not to be coerced into co-operation. Eschewing those alternatives as limiting cases and not co-operating will occasion entropic anarchy.

In this chapter two arguments, the latter emerging from a perspective provided by the former, will be considered. The first argument rehearses the "extremely high standards", to use De George's phrase, of legitimacy which anarchist sceptics demand of statehood. The sceptical argument rejects statehood on the grounds that a moral requirement of it is unrealisable as a result of which we are left with a logical rift between authority and autonomy and the moral priority of autonomy obliges us to reject authority. This argument is very much in the spirit of the quotation from Faure, above, and reasonably typical of anarchist attitudes. It will be reworked here because there is a practical, if slightly compromised, resolution to the conflict of autonomy with authority set up by the 'extremely high standards" of philosophical anarchism. The second argument outlines a political scheme in which authority and autonomy are reconciled and incorporated in an acephalous co-operative. The second argument will then be integrated with the idea of tuath and flesh out this model for practical anarchy.

I turn now to the first argument which is prefaced with a brief exposition of it. R.P. Wolff (1970) in his *In Defence of Anarchism* drives a sharp conceptual wedge between authority and autonomy.[2] He says that all states, by definition, claim the right to exercise authority (= demand obedience *per se*) but no autonomous agents can recognise as legitimate the rights of any external, e.g. state, authority over them. The one exception to this is where autonomous agents obey laws of which they themselves are author (unanimous direct democracy) in which case obedience to authority is permissible. Were unanimous direct democracy practicable in large scale, complex and multi-layered societies (such as most of us now live in), Wolff owns it as the *one* instance where, if it was incorporated in a state, that state would be legitimate. But, he adds, it is not practicable because a single dissenting voice breaks the unanimity condition and thus the basis of legitimacy. (In the second half of this chapter it will be argued that, with a very minor adjustment, the conditions of unanimous direct democracy can be met.) Wolff defends his argument for anarchy as a moral imperative on the premiss that autonomy is the primary normative principle and the rights claims of states flatly contradict the primary dictum. The consequences for political legitimacy are so considerable, if this turns out to be a well-founded argument, that it cannot be taken lightly. It would mean that every legitimate normative force propels us towards anarchism.

The state, according to Wolff (1970, p.3), is:

> ... a group of persons who have and exercise supreme authority within a given territory ... or over a certain population.[3]

Supreme authority is equivalent to sovereignty and sovereign action logically presupposes "the right to command, and correlatively, the right to be obeyed" (p.4). The matter in contention, so far as Wolff is concerned, is the claim that obedience could be used as the reason for acting. Obeying others for prudential reasons is another matter, he says. He uses the example of departing a sinking ship in which circumstance he is quite prepared to obey the "abandon ship" commands of the foundered vessel's skipper but only because he has reasons independent of the command for doing so, viz., he wants to survive the wreck and calculates his best chances are to be had from doing as the captain says. He would, he adds, be just as prepared to obey a fellow passenger if he thought that would maximise his chances of survival. To fix the point: obeying commands because they are commands is to accept authority. That is not the same as obeying commands because this action has instrumental value.

The unanimous direct democratic state is so contingently sensitive (one dissenting voice wrecks it) that it is too weak to withstand the inevitable pressures exerted upon a polity. It must be put aside. But all other forms of state claim authority on their own behalf. However, Wolff (p.8) goes on to say, they could be legitimate but if and only if:

> [W]e could demonstrate by an a priori argument that there can be forms of human community in which some men have the moral right to rule [issue commands].

But, "The fundamental assumption of moral philosophy is that men are responsible for their actions" (p.12). Furthermore, merely choosing to act is not the same thing as taking responsibility for one's actions. For an act to be responsible, the agent must have anticipated it with some deliberation, e.g. "gaining knowledge, reflecting on motives, predicting outcomes, criticising principles, and so forth". Thus:

> The obligation to take responsibility for one's actions does not derive from man's freedom of will alone, for more is required in taking responsibility than freedom of choice. Only because man has the capacity to reason about his choices can he be said to stand under a continuing obligation to take responsibility for them. (p.12)

In the interests of brevity this will be called his autonomy principle from now on. It is - let us be very clear on this point - incompatible with statehood:

> The defining mark of the state is authority, the right to rule. The primary obligation of man is autonomy, the refusal to be ruled. It would seem ..., that there can be no resolution of the conflict between the autonomy of the individual and the putative authority of the state. (p.18)

And, moreover:

> If all men have a continuing obligation to achieve the highest degree of autonomy possible, then there would appear to be no state whose subjects have a moral obligation to obey its commands. (p.19)

Of course, since state presences are now ubiquitous and they are all to some degree intolerant of dissidence, there are prudential reasons for complying with what they command. But this circumspect treatment of powerful - and dangerous - institutions is not equivalent to moral approbation.

Argumentatively, the weight of Wolff's imperatival call to anarchism rests on the conceptual purity of his authority/autonomy disjunction. One simply cannot have autonomy compromised by the presence of authority; bar the unique case of unanimous direct democracy, it is always a matter of one or the other. No direct challenge to Wolff's conceptual analysis is made here. However, something can be made out of its lack of empirical realism. Wolff's stipulated state is very peculiar in character; perhaps it is as much an ideal as his anarchy.

Admittedly the pristine conceptual scheme might help sort out the options intellectually but, in practice, there is something rarified about it. Perhaps with apologies to Wolff for the taint of compromise, the attempt will be made here to fabricate an anarchy in the spirit of his unanimous direct democracy which *a posteriori* falls short of his fastidious conceptual requirements. One result of this exercise will be the appreciation that the prospects for practical anarchy are not bedevilled by the the lack of empirical correspondence to the analytical authority/autonomy disjunction.

Consider two propositions (S) and (A):

(S) Subjects to them obey the commands of their states because they are commands of their states.[4]
(A) Individuals, by the principle of autonomy, are obliged, after due deliberation, to do as they think is (morally) correct.

Now imagine the following dialogue has taken place:

A: B, why did you do X?
B: Because the state commanded me to X.
A: Did you have any other reasons for Xing?
B: [truthfully]: No.
A: And everybody does as you do in your state?
B: Yes.

Evidently B's replies are consistent with (S) and both are part and parcel of the statehood which Wolff says we should reject because we are answerable under (A). There might be people like B outside the pages of H.G. Wells' *The Time Machine* but it is hard to imagine they are anything but rare, as rare as willing slaves whose mentality is moronic. Even in profoundly unquestioning societies, such as feudal ones in the Far East, the social psychology is not usually as simplistic as B's. True, the incidence of unquestioning obedience is extremely high but the motives for it are mixed: patriotism, personal (but not necessarily individualised) fulfilment, religion, fear of the consequences of disobedience, hope of reward, etc.[5] In other words the answer to A's first question, "Because the state commanded it" is usually a contraction of "Because the state commanded it and this is pleasing to God/will get me promoted/whatever". Moreover, as the level of political sensibility amongst the governed rises - as it did to a marked degree coincidentally with the development of capitalism in late medieval Europe - so does the expectation that there be decernable benefits in exchange for obedience. Hobbes' reasons for obedience to the sovereign are typical here: obedience is conditional on a balanced reciprocity. And, just as B's social psychology is strange to us so too is the (S)-type state. It is the very distillation of absolutism. The existence of states remarkably like this is not in question; there might well have been some such and conceivably could still be. However, other than the occasional defences of fascism and national socialism, there is nothing in modern political theory which comes anywhere near advocating an (S)-type state. On the contrary, almost the entire spectrum of modern statist political theory, from Hobbes at his most absolute to Nozick at his most conditional, is incompatible with (S)-type statism. Two points can be abstracted, for present purposes. The first (slightly mischievous) is that the way Wolff has cast the state makes practically all of us anarchists ... which might come as a surprise to those who, all along, thought they were liberal archists; on his terms rather a considerable number of archists (e.g. all those who obey states for reasons separable from the commands themselves) will be crypto-anarchists in fact. The second, obviously related, point is that, by making the state (S)-type, there is very little question but that Wolff's defence of anarchy is persuasive (though it does not follow that actual states are (S)-type). It is a possible moot point as to how far states which govern conditionally are touched by this conceptual analysis but that is not to the present point. What is being high-lighted here is that the very purity of its absoluteness makes the (S)-type state all but an abstraction.

At the same time this thoroughly sanitary analysis has been useful for throwing into sharp relief the tension between the autonomy principle and statist behaviour. It has also discarded something which might be worth picking up and having another look at - unanimous direct democracy. The remainder of this chapter does that. By borrowing and adapting an idea from Rousseau the attempt will be made to achieve a practical resolution of authority and autonomy which optimises autonomy and minimises authority. The result, if it works, will show how PIs, and others, can live *with* the endemic conceptual tension between autonomy and authority.

The state, as (S)-type, can be put to one side for the moment; it is a very special case. Nevertheless states do have (S)-type characteristics and a subject's refusal to obey is met with attempts at enforcement (threats, offers or throffers). (A) remains on the agenda. So too the question of how to get (A)-types to voluntarily co-operate where this move optimises their benefits. As they stand, their normative independence is effectively equal to that of Nozickian natural rights holders. It might be possible, then, that how Nozickians were handled will prove instructive for our treatment of (A)-types. To that I now turn.

There are, of course, many levels of co-operation possible from simple two-person, one-off activities to macro-social, long-term patterns of behaviour. This chapter is concerned with the latter; in particular with the need for and possible mode of legislative function in societies which do not have specialist, exclusive state organs to do the job. The task will be to show how, if at all, it is possible for individualists to obey only themselves and, at the same time, unite with the rest.[6]

To return to the *tuatha*: we already know the historical ones had customary law, passed down from one generation to the next. Presumably, too, the major social *mores* were likewise inherited and, whatever the dynamics of society, they did not greatly upset the widespread observance of traditional values. And we know that their assemblies met regularly but not frequently - annually, in fact. That plausibly suggests there were relatively few problems about co-operation of sufficient magnitude and unusualness to warrant much legislative activity. Looking back, or around for that matter, it is quite easy to believe that small-scale, traditional, homogenous societies, like those of Celtic Ireland, could indeed be acephalous without there being a need for much more than relatively informal, occasional political activity. But, simultaneously, this consideration might also present itself as a limiting factor on the applicability of this model to the often conflicting demands on legislation in macro-societies. Put another way: can the tuath's acephalous assembly cope with its job if its members do not share an inherited normative and regulative code? And, if it cannot, does not an invisible hand move society in the direction of archy?

To begin with a simple consideration: Nozickian PIs (of the less than ethically scrupulous order) can be expected to interfere with, if not wreck, the purposes of the assembly. All that is needed are the occasional free riders in the assembly who are looking for something for nothing out of the proceedings. If others in the assembly have their wits about them, they will realise they first have to bring the free riders to heel before they can deal with general business. But that might not be so easy. The wayward characters will try all means to defend themselves and, so long as they are successful, their efforts hold up and redirect the attention of the assembly from its proper concern with community affairs. However, such cases as these might not be particularly worrying. Technically, there are in place already lines of surety and filid law.[7] All the assembly need do is turn over to the filid those free riders who interfere with the purpose of assembly.

Even so, there remains a problem for the effective running of assemblies which results from a combination of circumstances: the absence of custom/tradition in that mode, the competitive nature of PI politico-economic behaviour and the assumption that our socio-psychological make-up is a fixed empirical datum. Successful political arrangements, it is often supposed, are those which come to terms with the constants in social psychology. This assumption, however, rests on mistaking a culturally specific social perspective for a general disposition. Contrary to that, the data of human history - and pre-history - suggest that, e.g. the belief that anarchy is equivalent to chaos is a product of a deep socialisation from within states. From within the stability of their existence as the *modus operandi* of politics, from one generation to the next, there has built up a dependency upon them to manage our collective affairs.[8] A point is reached in some minds where the alternative, voluntary political co-operation, is inconceivable. Part of the ambition in what follows is to show that the fixed perspective is mistaken. But to return to the point of detail in hand: Nozick thinks the invisible hand will begin to move society in a certain direction when individuals seek to protect their property (in person and goods). It has been agreed that could happen when we have nothing to go on but libertarian dispositions.[9] But now suppose agents in a state of nature have rather more political imagination than anarcho-libertarians. Say they can foresee that, without some kind of political concert, they are, indeed, in danger of falling prey to self-defeating anarchy. In a way they are moving towards a prudential regard for co-operation. It might be thought this is sufficient for them to find a way of moving beyond the reach of the invisible hand; it equips them with enough intellectual subtlety to see options. That, it will be suggested shortly is true but, at the same time, the matter is still delicately circumstantial. It is still possible, for instance, for such agents to become subject to the invisible hand - at a higher politico-cognitive level than Nozick's state of nature, as it were.

For the moment, let it be supposed, the free riders who tried to exploit the assembly have been removed. The remaining members of the assembly, being of a different moral stamp, do try to do the right thing, for all that they are liable to be handicapped on account of their (Nozickian) possessive individualism. The example I have in mind is slightly colourful, admittedly, but I hope it will illustrate the point. The assembly, having just ejected the suspected free riders, is now debating what to do *in general* with free riders. A general policy about them will be more economical, time- and money-wise, than having to deal with every case as a separate issue. It is mooted that such people should be ostracised, which implies a prohibition on association with them. But, some members of the assembly retort, that is a *boundary-crossing*: we all have a natural right to freedom of association and, if we are deprived of this then, in appropriate measure, we are to be compensated. Unfortunately, as things turn out, there is a deep and profound love relationship between one of the free riders and an assembly member. The assembly member bitterly rejects all the proffered compensation - nothing can make up for the loss of the right to freedom of association and his partner's companionship. Of course the assembly could suggest he be handsomely paid-off to join her in exile but, on Nozick's terms, he could still protest the moral impermissibility of this for it entails another boundary-crossing (his being sent into *de facto* exile) ... and two wrongs do not make a right. The normative tension generated by the efforts of the assembly and the demands of this member recreate a problem which Nozick found at a much more primitive stage in the state of nature. The assembly member has become, in effect, an independent and, moreover, favours his side of the contention with considerable passion - the sort of thing Nozick foresaw would polarise and, consequently, destabilise attempts to establish just procedures in the state of nature. The twist with this case is that PIs have *tried* to act within their permissible rights yet with those resources alone still seem in danger of degenerative anarchy. Without the midwifery of the invisible hand, political development[10] is still-born, we might say. At any rate that appears to be so when we are faced with the task of creating a viable polity, in contrast to, say, inheriting one such as the historical *tuatha*. But then *what* could have made the *tuatha* possible in the first place?

Much of the remainder of this chapter will inquire into how political authority could be constructed at the same time as a real intimacy between governed and government is achieved; the political distance between the two narrowed to a point of insignificance. If this can be done, without having to create a minimal state, a second foundation for viable acephalous polity will be in place. There will now be a legislative mechanism in addition to the legal one discussed in chapter 3 and the existence of both will owe nothing to invisible hands moving society towards a minimal or any other manner of state.

A legislative assembly acting on unanimous direct democratic lines is a *prima facie* likely candidate for anarchic community policy making. Serious and reflective anarchist philosophers agree but, at the same time, sound a note of pessimism as to its achievability. For instance Wolff writes (1970, pp.22-3):

> ... the solution [unanimous direct democracy] requires the imposition of impossibly restrictive conditions ... that is, a political community in which every person votes on every issue - governed by a rule of unanimity.

This is practical, however,

> ... only so long as there is substantial agreement among all the members of the community on the matters of major importance. Since by the rule of unanimity a single negative vote defeats any motion, the slightest disagreement over significant questions will bring the operations of the society to a halt. (p.24)

But,

> It is perfectly consistent with such a system that there be sharp, even violent, oppositions within the community, perhaps of an economic kind. The only necessity is that when the citizens come together to deliberate on the means for resolving such conflicts, they agree unanimously on the laws to be adopted. (p.24)

Reading those last two sentences in particular it is hard to suppress a Nozickian wry smile: how on earth are two people, who have just done each other violence, expected to sit down and *agree* as to what is to be done about it?[11] But that is beside the main point.

There is an element of danger about the predicament of the present argument. True, there is a law enforcement agency (the filid) but it is without regulative guidelines for its judgements; each individual lawyer is thrown back on the resources of her own judgement, presumably. That, however, is no great help in as much as, with nothing else to go on, the community is vulnerable to Nozickian decay. In the meantime, if what Wolff has just said about unanimous direct democracy is true, viz., a single dissenting vote is sufficient to scupper the efforts of the assembly in its efforts to co-ordinate voluntary co-operation in the matter of policy formation, then if anarchists look one way there is a rock and if they look the other there is a hard place.

Before finding a pathway out of that difficulty there is in Wolff's remarks a practical contention which, even if the major challenge before me could be overcome, would still blight the feasibility of unanimous direct democracy - as Wolff understands it. In order for the main argument to go forward unencumbered this subordinate matter will be addressed first, and dismissed. Every member of the assembly votes on every policy matter and without strict unanimity no resolution can be carried, so we are told. That, as Wolff says, is asking rather a lot. In the first place, it seems, people will be spending an inordinate amount of time just doing politics. Later I shall sketch out the case for and means of reducing the amount of political activity needed to sustain a community. That will overcome the first apparent problem. Except there is another aspect to it: what happens when the community - the whole community, remember - is in assembly? Do essential services like police, fire and emergency medical attention simply stop (in the middle of an emergency) to attend the meeting? What does anybody do who cannot get to the meeting (someone in hospital with both legs in traction)? Must the entire social and economic life of the community be interrupted? The picture is bizarre. But it certainly need not be the case and now even less so than ever before. This point was made by Wolff himself, in a later publication. With electronic communication being as comprehensive as it is, all who have business or other engagements which keep them away from the assembly can still register their views and votes through telecommunication. Indeed the whole business of the assembly could be conducted via this means. A simple computer (inter-net) controlled switching mechanism could fairly distribute air-time to all members, record their "presence", votes (if used) and so forth. The assembly has no need of a specific place from which to carry on its business - directness, anyway, is achievable. Well and good but we still have the matter of the single dissenting voice upsetting unanimity. There are at least two things which can be done about that (other than muzzling dissenters or some such illicit boundary-crossing) but since they emerge in the course of the main discussion that need be deferred no longer.

At the moment most states contain multi-cultural, multi-layered and multi-valued societies to one degree or another. In many ways this complexity of society is very enriching; it is even a conduit to greater - libertarian - freedom of choice, i.e. one can choose to move between layers in society, alternate one's preferences, etc. Simultaneously social complexity is a source of political tension, even downright contradictoriness ... and, apparently, it puts yet another burden on the very idea of unanimous democracy. Indeed, state governments, for the most part, have long since abandoned *laissez-faire* politics and no longer content themselves with keeping the peace. Instead, they give as much attention, if not more, to wrestling with welfare distribution logistics, financing their own very expensive operations and adjudicating competing demands from various, often conflicting, social and economic lobbies. So far as the last job goes Wolff (Wolff, Moore & Marcuse, 1985, pp.45-6), in describing the politics of the United States, captures its magnitude and its built-in unreliability (Nozick's sense):

... every genuine social group has a right to a voice in the making of policy and a share in the benefits. Any policy urged by a group in the system must be given respectful attention, no matter how bizarre. By the same token, a policy or principle which lacks legitimate representation has no place in the society, no matter how reasonable or right it may [sic.] be. Consequently, the line between acceptable and unacceptable alternatives is very sharp, so that the territory of American politics is like a plateau with steep cliffs on all sides rather than like a pyramid. On the plateau are all the interest groups which are recognised as legitimate; in the deep valley all around lie the outsiders, the fringe groups which are scorned as "extremist." The most important battle waged by any group in American politics is the struggle to climb onto the plateau.

75

Once there, it can count on some measure of what it seeks. No group ever gets all that it wants, and no *legitimate group* is completely frustrated in its efforts.[12]

Furthermore, it is far from unusual to hear statist government justified, or at least defended as the only option, on the grounds that it alone has the resources to carry out all the tasks expected of it. It might not handle things perfectly but at least it manages and contains the internally conflicting demands within its societies ... no pressure group is *"completely* frustrated in its efforts". And, if that is the best archy can do, with all its co-ordinated resources and funding from taxes, what chance has a voluntary co-operative community got? Surely we are back with degenerative anarchy?

The obvious answer is No. Just because statist governments do involve themselves in directing more than the peace does not imply they have to or even ought to. To be sure, if people expect government to manage security, the economy, welfare and arbitration then it might very well be imaginatively hard for them to picture a viable polity without the state. But there is the rub. I am reminded of Proudhon's observation that when monarchies were ubiquitous people could not imagine managing without them. Now states, though practically all are non-monarchic, have not collapsed in a welter of chaos on account of losing their monarchs. But the same can be said of states as Proudhon remarked on monarchies: societies, though managed at the moment by states, need not be necessarily. Possibility should not be confused with what can be imagined, least of all with the imagination of those who have long established patterns of thought and expectation.

I shall outline a mode of assembly which, though not unanimous in Wolff's very strict sense is, nevertheless, practically unanimous. This assembly will be the first modification needed to make the tuatha adapt to the demands which can reasonably be expected of it in the contemporary world. What is about to be outlined borrows generously from Rousseau though it is not to be understood from that that the borrowing will be a faithful reconstruction of Rousseau's politics. Rather, his ideas will be loosely followed. For instance, Rousseau distinguished two kinds of state: just and unjust with the former being comprised of those who, in obeying the law, are obeying what they themselves have willed. That I have and shall continue to regard as an aspect of practical anarchy or acephalous society, rather than a state.

The difference here is in nomenclature alone and does not raise any serious conceptual contention. The basis of the difference lies in my following Taylor where he says that a distinct feature of states is that, in them, legislation is a political specialism practised by a nominated number being less than the gross number of citizens within the polity whereas in anarchy it is a community affair, involving up to all members - which is exactly what Rousseau commends though, as I said, he nowhere styles himself as an anarchist.

Rousseau wrote (Levine, 1987, p.28):

> The fundamental problem of political philosophy, ... for which the social contract provides the solution ... is to find a form of association which defends and protects with all common forces the person and goods of each associate ...

That remark is unexceptional but it is followed by a reference to the means which make demands on political life very different from those of liberal democracy. The defence and protection in question are to be provided by:

> ... means of each one, while uniting with all, nevertheless obey[ing] only himself and remain[ing] as free as before. (p.28)

This could be promising, for an apparent normative gap is spanned such that individuals can contribute to collective enterprise without their individual freedoms being restricted. How, then, does this translate into legislative action?

Very briefly, all free actions have two efficient causes, if we follow Rousseau: a will to do it and the ability, or "strength" to carry it through (Rousseau, 1968, p.101).[13] In the case of legislative action, if this is to be consistent with the collective enterprise of individually free agents, the will must be general (the general will) i.e. the expression of the same proposition, severally and collectively declared. Let us say that when a proposition articulates the general will, the proposition is law. And, being law, the members of the tuath affected by it are subject to it. The move achieves a re-unification of government and governed. They are no longer different classes of agents; rather, they are different roles the same agents play. Other things being equal, it also achieves co-operation between members of the community without a structural need for coercion. It would be very odd indeed, having decided, as a matter of personal preference, that X (= the general will), is the best course of action to then not voluntarily X. And, thirdly, when their offices are called upon, the filid have law on which to base their judgements (by implication, too, judgements can be relied upon to draw from a public, common and disinterested code). In a way the filid are like Rousseau's executive or magistrates: they dispense the law. However, they are not entirely the same. The filid are independent agents, as we noted in chapter 3, rather than the executive branch of government or civil service. Of government Rousseau says (p.102):

> What then is government? An intermediary body established between the subjects and the sovereign [general will in assembly] for their mutual communication, a body charged with the execution of the laws and the maintenance of freedom ...

There will be occasion presently to note that, though this is a source of tension in Rousseau, it is not so in the tuath. But first: a frequently raised query about this scheme of things is, What about dissenting voices to the general will? Rousseau himself has tended to heighten the suspicion behind the question with such provocative remarks as, the dissenters will be forced to be free. But, in context, such claims are not as hostile to individualism as they might otherwise sound. Of course when there is no dissent in the matter of making a rule, R, then all citizens of the community, C, now subject to R are subject to their own wishes. The problem comes when some of C, C*, oppose R, even after all voices have been heard on the matter and debate seemingly exhausted. What next? For Rousseau the key question is: *why* are C* still antipathetic to R? If, e.g. R is for the general good and long-term self-interest of all community members and C* are figuring from a short-term, self-interested perspective then C* must be *forced*, in a sense, to see reason; they have to be argued out of their present, dim-witted perspective. That is, they must be brought to understand that everybody, including themselves, will be worse off in the long run if R is not initiated. But if, on the other hand, C* reject R because, say, it is flawed, it is a faulty means to the desired ends and not actually consistent with long-term self-interest, it is their job to make the rest of C understand the force of *their* argument. This toing-and-froing is the assembly *in* debate - not in resolution. It is important that debate is full, exploratory and open-minded. The purpose of debate is not achieved when one or another side has won; the purpose is that no "side" wins but all agree, having heard as much evidence and opinion as possible, that R is or is not in their best interests. A third possibility is that C* have not mistaken the best perspective from which to judge R but are, in fact, quite clear-headedly "on the make" for a free ride. In which case there is no doubt that Rousseau, in company with all the practical anarchists considered here, would expect them to be restrained. In that narrow sense it is possible for anarchists to subscribe to majoritarian measures to coerce the conformity of a minority to its will (or else ostracise it).

To bring the discussion back to its point of departure: Wolff's conditions for unanimous direct democracy are not satisfied to the level he demands by this manner of assembly. We have direct participation but not unfailing unanimity. That, however, does not undermine the polity. On the contrary; in, e.g. the case of the free riders, above, it strengthens it by ridding the community of socially malign presences.[14] The tuath now has a means of expressing its general will, of political community which yet meets the normative expectations of PIs (including, significantly, an extension of the concept of ownership for now the tuath members own not only their persons and material possessions but also their politics). In addition, this arrangement for the tuath has a number of consequential effects which add to its practical anarchic appeal. Four might be worth detailing.

The first ties into politics a very, very large contingent issue. I follow Geoffrey Warnock's (1968, p.12) understanding of the human predicament, namely that things are liable to go wrong.[15] The point of normative endeavours, including politics in its more reputable aspects, is to ameliorate this human predicament. Matters are liable to go wrong for a number of reasons. Firstly, because we have fallible understanding; we misread situations and/or respond to them in factually inappropriate ways. Secondly, we have conflicting wants and, obviously, when this results in some parties' wants going unmet, to that extent things have gone wrong (assuming that the wants are broadly legitimate). Thirdly, normative practices themselves are sometimes ill-conceived in terms of amelioration; some (fanatical and pathological) might be both evil and downright destructive, others, though benevolently intentioned, are muddle-headed. The human predicament makes it procedural folly to engage in normative action with anything more than conditional optimism as to outcomes. Politics is, tritely, the art of the possible; of far more moment is to appreciate the art of politics as the realisation of prudence.[16] Something interesting about estrangement occurs when we relate it to politics understood, in large part, as prudential response to the human predicament. Put it this way: there is the Platonic argument that it is only when politics *is* a specialism of the minds best equipped for it that we can hope to achieve the best from it, i.e. when it is categorically estranged from the governed. The best equipped minds would have to be ideally suited minds if this arrangement is not to entail very considerable empirical risks of exacerbating the human predicament. Less than perfect minds can boast no more than fallible judgement ... which is not a strong basis upon which to vouchsafe trust for the entire responsibility for lightening the human condition, let alone the even more demanding task of achieving the good life. Under fallible conditions the exclusion of people from political processes simply shrinks the pool from which we might recruit sound judgement. Generally speaking, the chances of countering the liability of things going wrong increase if we widen the demographic rate of participation in politics and deepen the understanding of participants. Dunn (1990) remarks:

> A modern political community ... would be a community which faced and accepted the need to judge and choose together, a community whose members are reared and educated on the premise that this was the responsibility which lay ahead of them at the core of adult life; this and not the opportunity to consume whatever pleasures prove to be accorded by their current market efficiency or made available to the dutiful citizen by the kind and provident ministrations of the state power.

Prudence, in our circumstances, requires a wide, participatory franchise. This brings in the point about estrangement. It has already been suggested that there might be a very high level of disaffection, of psychological dissatisfaction, amongst the governed when their relationship to government is very estranged. It can now be seen that, in addition, there is a practical inefficiency intrinsic to estranged government. Exclusive government limits its opportunities to exploit the full range of options open to it in policy construction. This is empirically imprudent, not to say gratuitously wasteful.[17] In order to maximise what might be called the politics of prudence, the nature of participation in the legislative activities of the community undergoes a change from what we are used to in liberal democratic states. It is tantamount to a shibboleth of modern democratic systems that political activity is a right; something citizens may participate in if they choose. But, for a variety of reasons - the limited number of public offices available, the sheer extent of estrangement, cynicism, torpor and so forth - the right is exercised by a fraction of state populations. The very nature of the acephalous community's assembly, however, rules out anything less than near consistent unanimous political participation. Indeed, involvement might have to be recast as a duty - rather than a right - a responsibility, as Dunn has just said.

An adjunct to what I have labelled the politics of prudence is that it encourages a sense of disinterestedness amongst members of the assembly. A reasonably clear-headed understanding of the human predicament makes people aware of the profound uncertainty of the future. People cannot count on the future serving their interests as well as their present fortunes do or they might wish them to. For reasons as capricious as they are beyond human control, the future can turn out to be a pleasant surprise or a nasty shock for all and any of us. Rawls talked about a theoretical veil of ignorance; there is, besides, a very real one. Humans *do* make decisions, undertake actions and legislate from behind a veil of considerable ignorance. Rousseau (quoted in Levine, 1987, p.53) understood this too:

> A thousand cases may arise for which the legislator has not provided, and to perceive that everything cannot be foreseen is a very needful kind of foresight.

As a general rule it is prudent to legislate sparingly for reasons of long-term self-interest, seeking the course most likely to have the highest pay-off within the broadest band of the vicissitudes of fortune. Planning under conditions of and for conditions of uncertainty has the nett effect of reducing partiality because agents have to hedge their bets against the future turning out to be a nasty surprise.

Consider, secondly, the requirement that legislation must be the expression of general will. This, too, encourages a frugal approach to legislative activity which, in turn, discourages the emergence of lobby and pressure group activity in the political domain. Perhaps this needs

81

teasing out. Premissed on PI, the reason for voluntary political co-operation is to ensure the peace and security of the community and its members, i.e. to maintain that good without which everybody is worse off. It is by assembly and its expression of the general will that this public good is distributed; there is no other purpose for political assembly. Furthermore, when political activity is extended, say beyond these spartan demands, there is the very real risk of it exposing normative differences within the community which makes the achievement of the general will that much harder, thus weakening the fabric of political community. The less demand for it, the greater the chances of achieving consensus, other things being equal. The tuath, as a political community, is going to be far less active than most statist political organisations which involve themselves in all manner of activities, as has been remarked above: the economy, welfare, the personal conduct of subjects, taxation, trading off lobbies, etc. Nonetheless, there will still be *partial* claims for the redistribution of goods - welfare claims, for instance. If these are not to be a concern for the assembly how are they to be managed?[18] Where the matter is of grievance of one party against another then it goes before the filid. Where, on the other hand, it is a matter of circumstantial distress, this can be managed through the *moka* system which is explained in chapter 6. In other words, the assembly has comparatively little work to do[19] and the nature of its work discourages (though does not render it immune to) attempts to use it for partial purposes. To the extent that partial pleading is suppressed by the nature of the assembly by so much, too, does the possibility for unanimity of general will rise.

Thirdly, the general reduction in commitment of time and effort to government is an economic benefit. To put the matter in crude terms: big government is expensive and, as Rothbard tirelessly iterates and re-iterates, the money for it comes out of the economy of the community - taxes. The material savings to be gained from "stripped down" governmental mechanisms reduce the aggregate disutility to society. This can be simply illustrated. Statist government as we know it has two main branches: legislative and executive (the civil service or Rousseau's magistrates). Perhaps from Hobbesian motives like self-glory, pride and power over others both branches of government have commonly developed over time material trappings "commensurate with the dignity of the office". That has cost the tax-payers money but not very much once depreciation is taken into account. The major burden of government upon the economy comes from financing its man-power. In developed Western economies the budget line for salaries is generally between 75-90% of the gross sum and this remains constant even when the personnel being paid are minimally productive. One invisible hand consequence of state governments managing more and more aspects of social life since the decline of *laissez-faire* government and its replacement with various welfare initiatives is that the civil service branch of government has grown enormously.[20] And, moreover, there has crept into the bureaucratic system a fiscal standard of "success". When the government budget is distributed to its departments those departments measure their prestige and their power to influence policy in terms of the relative sizes of their slices of the budget cake.[21] As a result of this practice government departments devote considerable determination and initiative to increasing their portion of the budget. Since they are all doing this there is a tendency for the aggregate demand on state finances to increase; that means pressure to increase the tax burden. Of course the pressure is not continuous - indeed, there are occasional efforts to reverse it - but it is continual. That is one reason why statist government is a financial liability to the community. Another aspect of statist government which makes it more expensive than the essentials of its functions require is that it is an establishment. It is paid on a retainer basis, not an operational needs basis. In market terms retaining an establishment even when it is "non-productive" (e.g. paying emergency services to sit and wait for something to happen) represents a nett, non-recoverable loss.

Polities based on voluntary co-operation entail operational costs, too. An obvious one is time spent in assembly matters is time lost to economic productivity in addition to the procedural costs of assembly business, e.g. providing facilities for it. But, after that, there are no significant budget items. Nothing like even a simple budgetary model is required to make the obvious point: acephalous politics costs the economy a microcosm of the sums entailed in maintaining statist governments (as we know them). And there is another form of saving which might be especially attractive to those who take no pleasure in politics: political engagement is far from burdensome. Quite the reverse: it leaves plenty of opportunity for the pursuit of other interests - whatever they might be.

Fourthly, Rousseau (1968, p.103) worried, understandably enough, about how the magistrates or executive would behave. When they behaved properly, then:

> The government [magistrates] receives from the sovereign [general will of the assembly] the orders which it gives to the [subjects]; and if the state is well balanced ... the power and the product of the government considered in itself should equal the product and power of the citizens who are sovereign in one sense and subjects in another.

Rousseau suspected that when the population of the assembly becomes great, individuals, finding less and less space for themselves in the debating of policy, are liable to a sense of political estrangement. In which case, executing policy requires more and more force. It is even possible that not only does the (now gross) assembly alienate citizens, it also becomes hopelessly muddled and bogged down in its own procedures. By degrees or by *coup* the executive might be tempted to take over the role of policy direction - simply to get things done. I agree with Rousseau that demography does have a bearing on the balance of the polity. However, he has more reason to be anxious about the magistrates than the tuath has about the filid. The thing is, in Rousseau's state, if there are magistrates with a higher than average interest in involvement in politics it is comparatively easy for them to "carve out" for themselves areas of political specialism and influence. Any mandarin knows that. This sort of activity is a serious threat to the power and authority of the assembly. The filid, because they are *not* part of government, are denied the access to the machinery of power which gave Rousseau cause for concern about his political structure. The tuath provides comparatively little opportunity for those who have a preference for political activity to use its structures as a means for developing a degree of political specialisation for themselves (which, of its nature, would skew the unanimity requirement).

In very broad terms, then, with the tuath's polity modelled on a Rousseau-esque assembly, the gap left by the absence of inherited law is filled without an anarchic community being moved by force of circumstance towards the state in order to keep the peace. At the same time the practical need for authority of a kind has been met.

There are costs consequential upon the development of what we might call political community in the tuath. I said earlier there are advantages to life in multi-layered, multi-valued, often internally contradictory societies. These actually provide a sort of freedom, e.g. of social and economic mobility. But, at this stage anyway, I cannot see a way for a tuath-based society being able to cope with the pressures of macro-scale, compound societies; the internal contradictions alone - quite apart from the enormous opportunities for free riding - are probably enough to decompose it to the point where the Nozick syndrome comes into effect. The nett result is, tuath anarchy becomes a political preference only if one accepts certain constraints on one's actions. The survival of anarchy depends in major part on *commitment* to its political objectives; opting out of what becomes, effectively, political responsibility opens the way to politics becoming a chosen specialism. And that is no more or less than another invisible hand move. However, such a lack of political responsibility is not very likely amongst anarchists who, after all, are motivated by a distaste for being under the will of others and/or have a moral preference for personal autonomy. For those who take the option of anarchy seriously the cost is more than worth it.

Another cost is that of being connected to lines of obligation and surety. This creates, as it were, a certain lack of privacy of action; it is in other people's interests to know what one is about ... and they will move to restrain one if one's intentions redound to their cost. But for whom would this be a high price to pay? Free riders, quite obviously. To a very large extent chapter 6 deals with this and related matters. For the present I simply state that crime, as a form of business, can expect to do quite well in multi-layered, multi-valued, internally contradictory states: it can exploit all these features very profitably. So much so that the occasional arrest is little more than a passing inconvenience. By contrast, the whole structure of the tuath militates against the success of organised crime as will be argued presently. So again, it seems, the cost is only a significant factor for such as have no interest in anarchy to begin with. This raises the possibility of another side effect: those who accept life in states for reasons of personal protection now appear to have a sound reason for preferring the tuath: security from crime in the tuath could very well be higher than it is in the state. If this is true there is a powerful irony in it. A rise in crime is often imagined to be the inevitable adjunct to anarchy - but what if anarchy is amongst the most effective barriers to the growth of organised crime?

If, in the foregoing pages, the argument that the tuath does have a means of governing itself without depending on a rich, shared and inherited culture on the one hand or needing political and service specialisms on the other has some merit, that is one thing; its theoretical viability is established. But, equally important is its resilience, its ability to withstand and survive hostile situations. Problems for it can come from within or without. Since this book is primarily concerned with the internal dimensions of anarchic communities the latter consideration will be set to one side, politically important in its own right though it is. But the question of resilience cannot be ignored altogether. Obviously the tuath must have some degree of functional robustness for there is little practical reason for erecting a structure which will collapse in the first breath of wind.

Imagine, then, some internal hiatus in the tuath. The situation is so vexed - whatever it is - that it appears to require legislative action for at least partial remedy. Let us say that the level of civic and political maturity in the assembly is very high and that on this occasion, as on others, the members are genuinely striving for the general will. Nevertheless their efforts are hampered by the scope and strangeness of the predicament confronting them and they find themselves at a stand with nothing achieved except moral polarisation. Rousseau, on whom so much of the argument has depended, is not much help here so far as the future of anarchy is concerned. He anticipated such an eventuality as is being considered and said that when it arises the executive branch of government must "silence all the laws, and suspend *for a moment* the sovereign authority" (quoted in Levine, 1987, p.53) and strategies for dealing with the emergency left to the government acting *ex cathedra*. There is no doubt that Rousseau desired that emergency powers be surrendered as soon as the crisis is past but he does not seem to provide any means to achieve this. Indeed there is a pessimistic anxiety in him that, once in power, the temptation to stay there might very well prove too much for the magistrates. Some critics (Levine, 1987) have found here a major flaw in Rousseau's thinking. It might equally indicate a measure of his intellectual honesty that he followed through his argument to its limiting point. Be that as it may, here we have to part company with Rousseau. Clearly it will not do for the fabric of the tuath's political system to be so weak that it tears at the first hint of a crisis. It will have to be made good if the tuath is going to stand as a resilient acephalous community.

In discussing reasons for the build-up of tension in the community and how it has been handled acephalously Michael Taylor offers a suggestion which the tuath anarchy can capitalise on. Taylor (1982, pp.135-6) writes:

> When a ... community ... grows too large for its members to work the local land, a part of it splits off and establishes a replicate community on new land. The same thing happens in cases of persistent internal conflict, the disaffected or unpopular faction moving out to establish an autonomous community elsewhere. This ... facilitates the maintenance of social order without a state, by removing sources of disorder and by keeping the community small enough for it to remain a true community, hence able to operate effectively the alternative social controls [which will be discussed in chapter 6].

As a report about the behaviour of acephalous communities - those few that survive - this is perfectly true. However, as a possibility for modern day tuatha it is quite out of the question, a critic might say. It presupposes there is unoccupied land to move to but, nowadays, the only unoccupied land is so because it is uninhabitable and even the limits of that are being pushed back under the pressure of a burgeoning human population. Fissioning, as this process is called, might have worked once but cannot now. It is hard to deny the brute fact - there is almost nowhere to go. And, on the face of it, some of Taylor's remarks do not seem to help either. For instance, he says at one point that where fissioning cannot occur and where social order is maintained only by internal means, we have the beginnings of statehood by force of circumstance (p.135). It would seem to be the end of the line ... except that fissioning to empty land is but one way of doing it; there are others besides. Suppose, for the sake of argument, the inhabited world is a mosaic of acephalous communities.[22] In addition - it is not hard to imagine - these communities manifest considerable diversity of internal value orderings and operations. If that is so, there is a very good chance that a group unpopular in this community will find itself quite well received in another tuath. Modern communications technology, in the form of universally accessible electronic data bases will be of great help here. If a group feels it is time to move on it simply accesses the library of information on other tuatha and chooses the most congenial. In fact the entire "immigration" process could be managed through this communication system so that, in advance of a fission, both immigrants and new host community are assured of their compatibility. Even in a crowded world, then, fissioning remains a possibility. It might even be easier now than it was the for Ancient Irish, given current and future sophistication of transport and communication resources.

The possibility of conflict, even when there is a widely shared understanding that long-term self-interest (which sometimes requires the suppression of short-term gains volitions) generates greater utility, is always present; it is part of the human predicament. However, so far the tuath has managed to escape that part of the predicament which moves it towards the minimal state and now it has managed to avoid Rousseau's dark vision of the recrudescent state. It has managed this by the fissioning procedure which effectively punctures those pressures which Rousseau, rightly from his point of view, both foresaw and feared.

I shall close this chapter by side-stepping one residual putative problem for anarchy but then foreshadowing how the tuatha will manage two others, viz. a system of justice (carried over from the discussion of Nozick) and economic management (carried over from the discussion of Rothbard).

First the side-step: there is a mild and well known joke which goes much as follows: a traveller in a foreign land is walking out one day. He comes across a local by the way and, wanting to know the route to the capital, asks the local for directions. The local thinks for a moment, then replies, "If I was going to the capital I wouldn't start from here". I have argued for the political viability of the tuath's assembly, for anarchic politics, on the premiss that government has the Hobbesian function of keeping the peace and security. But I have also mentioned the modern datum of multi-cultural, multi-layered, multi-valued, internally contradictory states. A frequent challenge to anarchic political philosophy is: if your political model could not manage these (bizarre) juggernauts it is out of contention because that is what it would have to do. At the root of this challenge is a logical mistake and in fact the juggernaut state is a spurious issue. Acephalous communities such as tuatha have no interest in managing such states; their case rests on being a radically different alternative form of society to them. The point of the joke becomes obvious: arguments for anarchy do not have to - perhaps should not - start by trying to cope with the problems and issues so central to the operations of contemporary states.

Of course a lot of anarchist argument starts with an expression of repulsion from juggernaut states as indeed did Faure's, quoted in the opening lines of this chapter. Alternatively, anarchism (as well as other theories) might be essayed with *a priori* exclusive rigour which is Wolff's approach. It might smack of weak-mindedness (weakness of resolution anyway) to those who prefer single, exclusive and majestic theories but so far my argument has only mooted tuath anarchy as an option; not *the* theory, just *a* theory. Though I shall persist in this feeble strain, nevertheless much of the effort in what follows goes into the attempt to highlight the appeal and viability of anarchy.

Secondly, the matter of justice: perhaps this should be re-worded to begin with because the concept of justice has been so enriched in modern political philosophy[23] that it now stands as a political landmark. What is in mind here is the far more humble use of the term to refer to the system for coping with free riders or criminals in general. So why not just say "the criminal justice system"? That would do except, for many, this is equated with "offences under state law" ... which of course is quite out of the question in the tuatha. Perhaps if a suggestion from Rothbard, which has already been referred to, is taken up it can be said that the topic in hand deals with criminality and justice understood in common law terms, i.e. logically independent of statist functions. There are two substantial points in this connection. One is that although the idea of the filid was traced in chapter 3 this was done in barest outline. What needs to be defended about it more rigorously is that a (mere) system of sureties is up to the task which states, for all the forensic ingenuity and sheer coercive force at their disposal, seem to be struggling with. The other is that the system of justice has its best chance of being effective when it is least used. Achieving that means extending PI perspectives to see the value of not only balanced but general reciprocity. With both those in place, it will be argued, circumstances militate against a high incidence of negative reciprocity.[24] Those points are the subject of discussion in chapter 6.

Lastly there is the question, or problem, of wealth. Taylor (1982, p.95) remarks:

Community ... clearly requires a measure of economic equality - a rough equality of basic material conditions - for as the gap increases between rich and poor, so their values diverge, relations between them are likely to become less direct and many-sided, and the sense of interdependence which supports a system of generalised and near generalised reciprocity is weakened. The economic equality that is a condition of community need be far from perfect: only gross inequality undermines community.

In chapter 2 something of a study was made of how gross inequalities of wealth can develop under libertarian anarchy. The question now before us is: could anarchic communities protect themselves from collapsing under huge wealth differentials? If so, how? Those questions are the subject of chapter 7.

Notes

1   See Wolff, R.P. (1970), *In Defence of Anarchism*, New York: Harper & Row, p.22.
2   Throughout we shall ignore the equivalence of 'authority' with 'expertise', e.g. X being *an* authority *on*/in chemistry/plumbing/ Ming porcelain, etc. The present concern is obviously with authority as in the claim to restrain or constrain legitimately the preference options of others. In a word, political authority.
3   This is not strictly true, however. Organisations such as the Mafia exercise supreme authority over certain territories and persons within states and are not themselves states. But there is no need to make an issue of that here.
4   A slightly imperfect example of this we could call the Nuremberg defence: if an agent A does x because A is ordered to, on some chain of command recognised by A, A does x legitimately. It follows, too, that A accepts no personal liability in having done x.
5   See Fairbank, J.K. (1988), *The Great Chinese Revolution 1800-1985*, London: Picador.
6   To paraphrase Rousseau. See Rousseau, J-J. (1968), *The Social Contract*, Cranston, M. (trans.), Penguin: Harmondsworth, bk. 1, ch.6.

7　Ignoring, for the moment, that in the absence of customary law and, supposing the assembly has handed down little or nothing by way of express law, the filid have little to go on. Assume, for the sake of argument, Common Law is more or less in evidence.

8　A point made by Taylor (1987, chapter 7).

9　This could be either an argumentative postulate or an empirical fact, e.g. the case of the Ik when external circumstances brought them to this condition.

10　That is bringing about sufficient co-operation to distribute indivisible public goods.

11　They might agree to a duel, perhaps, but that perpetuates rather than settles the violence.

12　We might note, in passing, that fringe groups would in fact be compensated in Nozick's MS provided, of course, they were not on the fringe by reason of perpetuating some illicit boundary-crossings.

13　The latter is of no importance to the present discussion. Nor, for that matter, is Rousseau's often colourful metaphysics. All that we need to note here is that a free action is (a) intended, (b) possible and (c) action because of (a) and (b).

14　Still another possibility is a genuinely unresolved epistemological difference about R between C and C*. In which case the practical alternative to the onset of consequential decay is for C* to fission. See chapter 6 for an outline of why fission is politically prudent and how it can be effected.

15　For a more detailed discussion of this see Edwards, P. (1985), "The Human Predicament: a Context for Rights & Learning About Rights", *Educational Philosophy & Theory*, Vol. 17, 1985.

16　I am indebted to John Dunn of King's College, Cambridge for this line of argument. See also Dunn, John (1990), *Interpreting Political Responsibility*, Cambridge: Polity Press.

17　These two reasons by no means complete the list. A major moral addition, which I have not included in the body of the text, is that justice, as fairness, requires democratic participation. See Rawls, John (1971), *A Theory of Justice,* Oxford: Clarendon Press.

18 It is a tacit implication of the argument in chapter 3 that *laissez-faire* indifference to such issues as welfare is at least prudentially risky. And, to be quite fair to libertarians, they do not entirely neglect these issues either, See, e.g. Rothbard's (1982) approving exposition of the Mormon welfare system.

19 That is in the normal course of events. Things might be different in an emergency, e.g. if the tuath is under attack or threat of attack by another tuath. In which case raising and maintaining an army will require rather more time in assembly.

20 Robert Peel introduced income tax in Great Britain as a *temporary measure* to meet the costs of the Napoleonic Wars. Not only has the tax never been repealed but it has steadily increased in mean terms ever since.

21 A point I owe to David Miller of Nuffield College, Oxford when strenuously but naively I was trying to defend the necessity for welfare politics.

22 Perhaps very much like the pattern of anarchic communities envisaged by Bakunin (1973).

23 Most notably by Rawls (1971) probably.

24 Terms which will be outlined presently. For a detailed account of them see Sahlins (1974) and Taylor (1982).

6 Responsibility & public order in acephalous community

States, the legitimacy of which is *not* maintained on theocratic, patriotic, ethnic or similar supervening normative grounds, are usually regarded as necessary to effect P-optimal pay-offs in public goods. They are needed to oversee, and enforce if need be, the co-operative moves - C,C - by the players in a Prisoners' Dilemma matrix. This form of reasoning generally assumes that people are dispositionally PIs seeking as near immediate gratification of their ego desires as possible. Such creatures, left to themselves, will always (so the argument goes) fall victim to the Dilemma. P1 will play D for at least one of two reasons: (a) the even chance of P2 being foolish enough to play C, giving the result 4,0 and (b) believing that if he plays C, P2 will naturally play D, resulting in 0,4. P1, having played D, leaves P2 with no reasonable option but to play D, too, the resulting pay-offs being 2,2, say, which is, of course, P-inferior. P1 and P2 can only be counted upon to play C,C, thereby achieving the P-optimal 3,3, if they are forced into co-operation. *But* that force has to be operated by an agency exogenous to P1 and P2. In political societies such as we are familiar with, it is the state which is expected to operate that force. If we follow this broad pattern of argument we can readily appreciate why Weber's definition of the state (Taylor, 1982, pp.4-5), viz. states are "associations that successfully claim the monopoly of legitimate use of physical force within a given territory", is so widely accepted. Aside from its refreshing brevity, it encapsulates the idea that the state may *rightly* force P1 and P2 into co-operating. The state appears to be an objective requirement for civil society. True, there might be subjective feelings of irritation with states from time to time, say when people have to pay taxes to them, but that they are necessary just is so. All that remains to discuss is what forms and procedures states may (normatively rich sense of "may") adopt. Not for the first time, I come back to the observation that the last sentence captures the limits of much, if not most, contemporary political theory. Heterodoxy as to forms of state there undoubtedly is but that we have to have a state of some sort to regulate behaviour in order to safeguard the distribution of public goods is seldom questioned (and then only by anarchists).

The focus of attention thus far has been on the political forms of anarchies as means of achieving co-operation at the legislative level. However, as indicated at the end of chapter 5, this chapter will concentrate on co-operation at the level of personal responsibility for actions which have effects on other members of the community. To be more exact: what is to be done about or with agents when they do *not* co-operate and this materially contributes to a violation of public and/or private security? For the purposes of the discussion to follow three broad categories of non-co-operation, of a criminal kind, will be considered. These are organised crime, crimes of personal violence and political crimes. Discussion can be prefaced by a brief outline of each category. Organised crime is really criminal activity as a form of commercial enterprise. It can very often draw on the other two categories but its main purpose is to make money for its perpetrators. Protection rackets and other forms of extortion might, *prima facie*, get a toe-hold in the tuath.[1] Crimes of personal violence have already been mentioned, in chapter 2 where, it was noted, these turned out to be one of the two manifestations of crime recognised by Rothbard. Personal violence is self-explanatory though, it must be admitted, there is a vague penumbra. Mental injury can be inflicted, of course, but what counts as mental injury seems to admit of considerable variability. However, that violence against persons is manifestly possible and prohibited on both rights-based and deontological grounds is beyond doubt. Thirdly, political crimes: a sub-heading which might at first glance appear to be outrageous in the context of a defence of anarchy. In fact it is not. For instance, if an agent, A, were to try to establish hegemony over an acephalous community, C, then it would appear uncontentious that C has a case against A for a political crime.

Up to this point there has been very general talk about the problem of free riders, those out to get something for nothing from the community. The three categories of criminal activity distinguished in the previous paragraph are forms of free riding in that by committing them gains are expected to be optimised without there being any attempt at balanced reciprocation (though minimal reciprocation might come into the calculation). In the case of organised crime there is a barely recognisable reciprocity when, say, the protection gang (a) does not itself vandalise shops "on its patch" and (b) reduces the risk to those shops from outside gangs. In that case the ride is not utterly free ... but certainly the next best thing. Straightforward theft (in all its particular forms) is a paradigm free ride. Crimes of violence, when they are not means to other ends (such as organised crime), are not so obviously free rides. Nevertheless, a case can be made for them as such. If agents are somehow satisfied, say psychologically, by doing violence to others and seek to evade any reciprocal consequences then those agents are attempting a free ride: satisfaction at the expense of others at no cost to themselves is free riding. The same goes for political crimes. And in this case we can actually make some useful distinctions. For example we can distinguish a *coup d'etat* from a revolution on the analytical basis of free riding. The former is a free ride because it is the effort to gain the benefits of political power for one's own ends (and if anybody else benefits that is purely contingent on who needs to be "bought" for tactical purposes). On the other hand, a revolution is in the name of a class or cause and the cost of revolutionary activity is borne selflessly to some degree.[2] But, to round off this very brief analysis with a general point, not all free riding is criminal. Some forms of gambling, as we shall see in a minute, are understood as free riding but, in anything less than strictly puritanical circles, gambling is not considered criminal.[3] Free riding and criminality, therefore, are not equivalent. In the context of the present argument there is the concomitant that restrictions should only be placed on free rides which are criminal in PI terms, i.e. those rides which are inside the rights boundaries of others. But, with that proviso in mind, I shall use the terms interchangeably in what follows in order to avoid tedious repetition of the same phrase.

How, then, does the tuath control free riding? Firstly, in contrast to states, anarchic community possesses a minimum concentration of force and political specialisation (Taylor, 1982, p.33). It appears to be singularly ill-equipped, then, in that it has no established police prevention, detection and apprehension service. Granted it has the filid which will hear cases but what is to be achieved by that when there seems to be no device to bring accused before the courts in the first place? That question is partly idle in that how it can be answered anarchically has already been indicated in the reply to Nozick on this very point in chapter 3. However, an indication of how a challenge can be answered is not the same thing as a full answer to it. That will now be attempted.

In *viable* anarchies social order and security are maintained by one or more of three means. These are, (a) "social controls proper" which include threats, offers and throffers. A throffer is a combination of threat and offer, e.g. if A does not do x, he is threatened with punishment p; if, on the other hand, A does x he is offered reward r. It is clear that throffers are usually more potent means for the control of free riding than mere threats or offers. (b) The "process of socialisation" which has the effect of shaping, moulding and limiting the range of agents' preferences; our up-bringing disposes us to like this, not that and so forth. (c) The "basic structural characteristics" of societies such as kinship patterns, modes of competition and co-operation and the division of labour. Obviously, any or all of these can be, and usually are, features of life in archic just as much as anarchic societies. The difference between the two, Taylor (p.66) says, is that the latter have, in addition, features of reciprocity, fissioning and widespread crossing-cutting of relationships.

Reciprocity is an aspect of anarchy which has only been mentioned so far. It is now time to give a more detailed explanation of what is meant by it here. On Taylor's (pp.2-31) understanding, without it, it is practically impossible to achieve optimal utility voluntarily. A particular feature of Taylor's use of the concept is that it is a combination of short-term "altruism" and long-term "self-interest" such that: agent A helps B now in the vague, and not necessarily economic, expectation that B will help A in the future. "Altruism" here has the relatively spare meaning that A's present act costs him and benefits others, B in this case. However, it does not mean that A "writes off" the cost as a loss; when needed for some reason, A counts on B for help. In a relatively stable society, not faced with a major disaster such as the Ik were, the number of "favours owed" will exceed the number called in. Thus the typical long-term effect is to raise the stock of public, available utility; with widespread cross-cutting of relationships everyone is probably owed more than they have paid out. That is one feature of reciprocation. Following Sahlins, Taylor says another is that reciprocity occurs on a continuum, the two ends of which are "generalised reciprocity" and "negative reciprocity" and the mid-point "balanced reciprocity". Hospitality, help and generosity are examples of the generalised form. And if, say, B who is in trouble is helped by A, then the flow of goods from A to B might be pretty much one-way for a while. The direction of flow is circumstantial, however; at some time and somehow B is expected to reciprocate, though not necessarily in kind. Balanced reciprocity involves direct exchange. Trade, be it of goods for other goods or a cash economy, is of this kind. The flow is a near immediate two way process. If that temporal proximity of reciprocation is jarred - if, e.g. one's ability to pay is in question or one actually defaults - the system breaks down. Negative reciprocity is another term for free riding - theft, obviously, but Sahlins includes as other examples haggling and gambling interestingly enough (Taylor, 1982, p.29). Negative reciprocity will not sustain community or, in the long term provide little, if any, individual or public utility.

States play a considerable role in attempting to prohibit, or at least restrict, negative reciprocity and, largely through their civil court systems, they supply redress where balanced reciprocity breaks down. Generalised reciprocity is not normally regarded as the responsibility of liberal states though in highly socialised and/or welfare states particular forms of generalised reciprocity are within the purview of the state, e.g. the state propaganda campaigns in post-Liberation China designed to raise the level of individual contributions to the general good for no immediate or ostensible personal gain. The revealing point of comparison about reciprocity in liberal states *vis-a-vis* communities is that, though it is not central to the function of the former to *promote* generalised and balanced reciprocal relationships (though they might essay protection of balanced reciprocity), the promotion of both is a source of resilience in the latter. There is practically an equation here: the (prudential) need for archy rises in proportion to the degeneration of reciprocity (excluding negative). That was Nozick's point, with the rider in his case that the quotient of degeneration need only be very small before the state is required to rescue people from self-defeating anarchism. But, as has already been pointed out, this does not mean that states, minimal or otherwise, are inevitable. We could argue, rather, that if members of a community have an interest in its welfare, they *have* to do something about it (otherwise the invisible hand might very well sweep it away). Of course constant vigilance against moral backsliding, with every member watching all the others (hopeless task), is not the sort of interest required. Rather, this is where the basic regulative structure of a society and its processes of socialisation come into play. In combination these reduce the incidence of and contain the effects of any tendencies towards negative reciprocation. I shall indicate how.

It will be remembered that the tuatha comprise, in part, intricate kinship patterns. Actually, they do not have to be *that* intricate just so long as the ramifications of liability discourage people from exposing themselves to suite. The difference between our modern, Occidental sense of family, say, and that of the tuatha is mainly this: for us being a family relation - except, perhaps, spouse, parent or child - carries no serious expectations. To be sure, we are supposed to like our siblings, for instance, but many people do not and that is an end to the matter so far as anybody else is concerned. In the tuath, on the other hand, being related by family might very well be the beginning of the matter.[4] Thus, if A, who is related to B1...Bn, steals from C and absconds with the proceeds, B1...Bn will find themselves liable, under filid law, to compensate C for the losses. This system has something of the appearance of strict liability in modern statute law: one is held responsible for an event which one's movements or circumstances brought about whether one could help it or not. But our sense of fairness might be offended by this. If we are blameless for an event why should we pay the costs? The tuath members also have a sense of fairness; it is just that their perspective is different. They say it is unfair to C that she be robbed and a fair equilibrium is only restored when she has been compensated. The fact that there are two ways of looking at fairness here, as opposed to thinking one system fair and the other not, is vital. Were it the case that the filid system just is unfair that would nullify its chances of being accepted as a legitimate feature of the pathway to anarchy. Fortunately this is not the case. Consider: in modern (British) law, with no exceptions I can think of, if C is robbed by A and A successfully hides the goods, whether he is caught or not, C cannot expect to see her goods again or be compensated for their loss (unless C is insured ... which she herself has paid for anyway). That is unfair; arguably quite as unfair as A's relatives being required to compensate for his crime. We can at least say that filid law is no more unfair than ours - it is fair and unfair in different ways. With that possible bind out of the way, we can now look to other differences. Some of them might show up considerable advantages in the tuatha's sense of "extended responsibility". Lines of extended responsibility have, firstly, a heightening effect on our sense of responsibility for our own actions and, secondly, a policing effect on the actions of others without the need and cost of an establishment force. Suppose I am tempted to rob you. Today, in a crowded street in London or, perhaps, a darkened one in New York I could easily part you from your wallet being sure that *nobody* save you, me and, maybe, the police could care less. I could not be so sure in a tuath. Even if I could not be found, having stolen your wallet, any information linking me to its wrongful possession is going to link those in my line of extended responsibility and surety. For a number of possible reasons that might very well discourage me from stealing in the first place. Such reasons could be: I happen to like my kin and not want them to suffer on my account; I believe it contrary to the code of decent behaviour to implicate kin; I fear what they will do to me when my kin catch up with me; I am liable to public ridicule and shaming. Modern forms of generalised, high-speed communication make the latter a potent force. Any one of these, and perhaps other reasons, will contribute to raising my sense of responsibility for my actions. Secondly, the policing effect (though this has all but been dealt with in chapter 3): none of us with any common-sense and having extended liability is going to let people in our line lumber us with their crime debts. We are simply going to discourage crime in our line. The nett effects of this social structure upon the incidence of free riding within the community are: (a) we can expect its occurrence to be very low[5] and (b) there will be negligible policing costs to the community because liable lines will have powerful interests in doing that job themselves (without being a burden on the public pay-roll). In sum, the system is its own means of keeping up the level of interest in its wellbeing - to neglect one's co-operative responsibilities entails a liability to negative reciprocity which, in turn, will be very costly. Here, on the economy and reliability of security, as in other aspects of anarchic life, there is concert with Rothbard's description of it.[6]

Thus far, then, the matters of detecting and reporting free riders have been considered. That leaves out of account a frequent source of scepticism about the viability of anarchy, viz. its lack of coercive means sufficient to exact compensation for wrong-doing (theoretically a line of liability might never pay the bill; as each one in line is presented with it, she simply passes the buck). In sum, few doubt the possibility of law in acephalous society, rather more doubt it will be effectual. Something of the sceptical view has already been discussed in chapters 3 and 4. But, to refresh memory and elaborate a little: assume for the sake of argument that most people do as they ought. Nevertheless, we can expect two kinds of problem. Firstly from those who are criminal. Secondly, from other free riders, people who benefit from there being public goods but who contribute nothing to their provision. Of course people might not be allowed to do these things but, without a specialist branch of government to restrain them, how otherwise are criminals and other free-riders to be controlled? It is all very well to say that filid law and extended lines of liability are going to control crime, but are they? Filid regulations might inhibit amateurs, kids doing it for kicks and similar lightweights but what of professional criminals, people who are in it for a regular source of income (our first broad criminal category)? It requires no stretch of the imagination to see that, in all probability, those who are in crime as a serious matter of business will, in fact, absorb their liability lines into the business. Control over the liability line is then likely to shift. The "godfather" will regulate a crime network with just the same devices as a state or autonomous community: social controls proper (such as throffers, threats and offers), a basic hierarchical (government/governed) structure and processes of socialisation (learning, often in a sort of osmotic way) what is done and not done. An acephalous community, if it has any goods of value to the godfather, is likely prey to him. Surely, the obvious thing for the community is to buy security specialists ... thus could the invisible hand make its first Nozickian move.

For resisting the invisible hand here Taylor (1982, p.91) offers a number of choices other than the purchase of specialist coercive forces. Again drawing on anthropological precedent he cites withdrawal of reciprocity, public ridicule and ostracism. Possible, too, though perhaps somewhat outmoded, are threats of witchcraft and supernatural invocation. Imagine, for a moment, the godfather's "mob" moving in on an anarchic community (with the necessary historical adjustments, a phenomenon by no means uncommon, e.g. during the period of European expansion and consolidation in the history of the United States of America). The question then is: has the acephalous community the means to withstand the take-over? On the surface, it does not look like it. For a start, the dispersed network of liability lines, though it might have effect within the tuath's system, appears useless now because the threat is from without, not within it. There are warriors in the tuath who, as we know, fight irregular, low key and (most important) low cost skirmishes with neighbouring tuatha. Unfortunately, in dealing with a tightly disciplined organisation which makes profits from violence, there is precious little chance of sporting warriors having much success. Thirdly, withdrawing reciprocity, public ridicule and ostracism are not only idle threats but attempting them against the mob is plain dangerous. In brief, surviving, let alone resisting, an invading mob is a very remote possibility. The mob, it seems, can only be handled with a like or superior force in kind.

Something has gone wrong with the story, however; it has slewed off the point. The mob, in this example, is the same in all relevant respects to any other invading force such as a foreign army or whatever. The point I began with was: can the tuath handle crime? But I have now asked a different question: can the tuath resist invasion?[7] We have to think about a "home grown" mob, if the first question is to be answered. And, of course, if the mob's infrastructure is well developed then it might well simply absorb the tuath. As Rothbard remarked most, if not all, states had their origins in the mastery of brigands. But are there not structures and processes within the tuath which militate against the development of the mob? What about the process of socialisation? I take it that this solemn sounding phrase refers to the up-bringing of the community's young, to their nurture in their families and their schooling which result in them identifying themselves and being recognised as members of that community. Presumably a measure of the success of socialisation is the extent to which community members have regard for its normative beliefs and processes and revulsion (cognitively and affectively) at what the community takes to be morally wrong. That is certainly true of small communities. It is also true to a surprising degree in large, complex and multi-layered societies. Even in something as otherwise fragmented and heterodox as the capitalist world, the attachment to capitalist economics and ideology and hostility to anything styled communist or communistic is almost universal. In that case it becomes perfectly plausible to assume that the social fabric and its processes will simply be inhospitable to the growth of mobs. People will take more interest in curtailing their emergence than encouraging them. Furthermore there is no obvious economic incentive to develop one: apprehension for criminal activity - which a large number of people (the entire liability line) have deep personal interests in - means restitution of all costs. And the costs are restoration of goods stolen, plus payment for any damages, plus gross legal fees. When profit is the motive for crime the combination of these factors is a far bigger disincentive than, say, serving a gaol sentence (and still having the proceeds of crime to live off after release). Thus, our answer to the sceptic is this: the tuath has a different approach to crime. The idea that we have to have enforcement and punitive measures tacitly implies that crime is endemic; to be discouraged, yes, but, sadly, with us anyway. There is even a sense in which it can be regarded as the extra-legal aspect to the economy. The tuath, with its emphasis on socialisation and heightened sense of social responsibility shifts the balance from management to prevention. Rather than the buck being pushed down the line, it is pushed up ... to the miscreant. The community's dynamics make free riding a very unattractive proposition. So unattractive that the emergence of anything like organised crime could only occur if, for some reason, the community was in the grip of profound malaise (as the Ik were).

But there are still personal violence crimes, usually the infliction of bodily harm, which are not committed for economic gain. Surely, the merely civil process of filid law is ineffectual against these? Even the withdrawal of reciprocal relations is not an obvious means of inhibiting these offenders. Taylor (pp.65-90), however, points out that in earlier societies, e.g. hunters and gatherers and closed peasant communities, ostracism was a powerful means of control. On the one hand it was a very palpable psychological disincentive to offend for it meant the loss of all benefits of society, both material and affective. On the other hand it was a very effective, not to mention cost efficient, form of social hygiene. The community simply rid itself of those beyond the pale of its tolerance. We can certainly see how the system could work in small communities where everybody knows everybody, their business and their whereabouts. Yet for the vast majority of humanity the circumstances of life are very different from that. So much so we now talk of the ease with which we can become lost in the crowd. This is surely a very agreeable environment for violent criminals: plenty of victims around and, even if caught and expelled by the filid, who is going to find offenders when they sneak back in, merging anonymously into the mill of people? Oddly enough, it is precisely in this modern world where ostracism could become a truly effective - and terrifying - sanction. The key to this is telecommunication systems. Imagine A, a convicted violent criminal, is ostracised from place X. A's details of identity and conviction are keyed into a sort of super-Interpol communications and data-base network which is global. The world now knows who A is, what his history and circumstances are and how he has offended. Then he is forced to leave X. But, nobody else, anywhere, will let him stay. He is condemned to a Kafka-esque existence, marked and rejected no matter which way he turns. I have no interest in commending this treatment of criminals. It is merely indicated here to show how community-based punitive modes, far from being arcane, can be more effective than ever before in the modern world.[8]

Political crimes, the third category distinguished above, could be managed by ostracism, too. The-mechanism will not be fail-safe - certainly no more so than most social mechanisms. However, in conjunction with the other circumstances of anarchy, in particular the lack of any centralised means of force, the dispersed public media forms of communication, the lack of integrated means of public surveillance, etc., the chances of even organising something approximating a *coup d'etat*, let alone getting it under weigh are remote. The situation is not conducive to large scale political free riding. However, prejudicing the course of debate in the assembly, poisoning the well and otherwise undermining open politics is possible in an acephalous community. That, however, is not a liability unique to anarchy; it applies just as much to archy so, strictly speaking, it is not a matter in contention here. And, besides, when this sort of activity occurs the assembly need lose no time in handing the miscreants over to the filid.

Above, I have tried to give some idea of how the tuath's filid system can operate effectively against crimes of profit, violence and politics without the need for security becoming an instrumental specialism or ultra-minimal state.

However, a problem might arise here. I have said the greater the incidence of specialisation in government-type functions the higher the risk of estrangement of government from governed. Now take the case of filid law. The filid specialise in interpreting law, and adjusting it to cope with altered circumstances, hearing cases and handing down judgements. Further, because the practice of law is the only governmental function (Rousseau's sense) in the tuath, do we not have a clear case of estrangement of government from governed? And is that not a very obvious movement towards the development of statehood? If so the tuath serves ill as a paradigm for stable anarchy. The difference between a state and a tuath depends on a fine distinction which I shall now try to draw.

In chapter 2 we found Rothbard commending the virtues of court processes as forms of business enterprise. Those in dispute and wishing to have their dispute settled would "shop around" amongst those who make this sort of work a specialism. The filid are, in fact, just such people. They survive in the market because they are valued for the quality of their work and the consequent trust people place upon it. Theirs is a professional relationship to their clients, i.e. it is voluntary, balanced reciprocation of fee for service. If either fee or service are found wanting, the relationship is severable by either or both parties. In sum, the filid function on a supply and demand basis of legal expertise and judgement. The jural system in a state also supplies legal expertise and judgements and it, too, is paid for its professional time. That is where the similarities end. Archic criminal justice systems have, under law, responsibilities for prosecution and unilateral powers of intervention (within law). Prosecution is not contingent on clients engaging their services and, concomitantly, they are not remunerated by clients, they are retained by the state and every tax-payer contributes to their upkeep (with no reference to voluntariness, obviously). The filid serve clients, on individual contracts bases. Thus, because jural process in the tuath is civil it really makes no sense to think of it in governmental terms. We are only liable to suppose otherwise if we have a conceptual carry-over from Rousseau, viz., that government executes the general will upon subjects. There is no such intermediary, governmental function in the tuath. The work of the assembly is the only political function here. After that it is anybody's right to prosecute a case in law ... but nobody's responsibility.

Even so, what if, say, filid Y became so popular that this firm gained a monopoly? Is not the result an embryonic state not dissimilar to Nozick's DPA? The answer is, it is very similar though just because we have a combination of conditions which could lead to the evolution of a such-and-such, this does not entail that such-and-such will evolve.

True enough; nevertheless the possibility cannot be lightly brushed aside here because a PI monopoly on the legal/protection system of its very nature destroys a vital acephalous quality of the tuath. The question, then, seems crucial to the argument that the tuath is a viable, sustainable and stable anarchy. It must be answered. It is crucial not in the sense that if it cannot be answered with a closed reply then the argument for the viability of the tuath is doomed. No, it is crucial in that, partly because the answer to it is open-ended, it helps us understand where the limits of anarchy's viability are to be found. There is no pretence in this argument that the pathway to anarchy being opened up is not liable to be washed out. Indeed, there is a parallel between the circumstances of Rousseau's just state being taken over by the magistrates and the kind of threat presented to the tuath (or, worse, the tuatha) by a consolidated monopoly of the filid. In either event it depends on the reaction of the members of the community as to what happens next. If the members of the community have a committed hostility to this in all but name DPA there is every likelihood of violence; anarchy starts to degenerate and Nozick's invisible hand comes into play. If, on the other hand (however unlikely) the community capitulates without demur to the DPA then there is no call upon the further activities of the invisible hand. Either way, the point is a simple one: if there arises a monopoly on governmental-type powers *there is no practical anarchy*. Furthermore, all acephalous communities are "at risk" from this; but, to paraphrase Taylor, that is not an argument to the effect that anarchy *will* succumb to the invisible hand. At the same time it goes without contention that immunity to risk is only partial.

Notwithstanding the admission of a structural delicacy in the above paragraph, the tuath's filid system, provided it remains just that, along with its peripheral supports, e.g. socialisation, is sufficient to contain the problem of free riding within manageable limits. It is doubtful if crime will be eradicated altogether but the life of the tuath does militate against the profitability of crime and crime for kicks has consequences too horrifying to be seriously considered by more or less stable minds.

There is one fact of social life which is conspicuous for want of treatment so far, however - wealth. Rousseau regarded equality of wealth as very important to the viability of community. Taylor (1982, p.95) echoes him:

Community ... clearly requires a measure of economic equality - a rough equality of basic material conditions - for as the gap increases between rich and poor, so their values diverge, relations between them are likely to become less direct and many-sided, and the sense of interdependence which supports a system of (generalised and near generalised) reciprocity is weakened. The economic equality that is a condition of community need be far from perfect: only gross inequality undermines community.

In chapter 2 an example of how inequalities of wealth could arise was amplified and some of the social and moral consequences were outlined. However primary states did, in fact, develop aside for a moment, it can be seen why a powerful trend in both the liberal and socialist justifications for the state are that it is needed to curtail the emergence of the peon relationship. It is a line of reasoning which can be traced from Rawls back to Hume. The question now before us is: could anarchic communities protect themselves from collapsing under huge wealth differentials? If so, how?

We could begin by looking at precedent acephalous communities.[9] However, it is doubtful if we could develop much of a general argument from that for the simple reason that developed economies are different from many traditional ones. Developed economies create surplus as an essential feature, traditional economies can be undermined by it. A modern acephalous community's economy is going to have to manage surplus, in all likelihood, and somehow stall propulsion towards the peon relationship. By its very nature the peon relationship fractures any cohesion a community might have had, raising in its stead two economic classes. *Prima facie* a communist approach might serve insofar as we dove-tail the ideas of the withering away of the state with (rough) equality of wealth to provide a structure resistant to the development of exploitative relationships. This will be explored in the next chapter.

Notes

1   As to whether narcotics distribution, gaming and prostitution rings could is arguable. On the face of it there is a very strong chance that an anarchic community will not prohibit any of these activities in which case it follows as a matter of logic that they could not be

areas of criminal activity. On the other hand, of course, there is nothing to stop an anarchic community from having a puritanical streak to it.

2   Putting aside, for the moment, such complications as compromised motives.

3   Examples of puritanical laws which criminalise gambling which I have in mind are those of Saudi Arabia and the People's Republic of China.

4   A line of obligation along blood lines is not the only possibility, obviously. Sureties could be based, say, on economic guarantees or some form of social affiliation (e.g. a lodge) or these and other things besides in combination. The nature of the line is not important; what it can do, is. Blood lines have been chosen to illustrate the point here because they are so familiar in our lives anyway.

5   Psychopathically induced events will still occur but might reduce to the extent that families will mind their lunatic members better. Crimes for profit will decrease.

6   This is not a contradiction of the argument in chapter 2. There I was concerned to highlight a normative deficiency in his argument for anarchy. But, in the time-honoured cliche, there is no useful purpose in throwing out the baby with the bath water. Much of Rothbard's description of how public utilities and welfare goods could be provided for without a state - a separate matter from his argument for anarchy - is logistically feasible and quite attractive.

7   As a matter of fact the historical tuatha *did* successfully resist invasion to a remarkable degree. See chapter 3, above.

8   This leaves out of account violent people disposed to run amok. Surely, in this case, there is a need for incarceration to protect the community from attack; ostracism merely means somebody else, over there, is now endangered. Not necessarily; it is just as possible to shut people out as lock them in. Exactly how that is done seems to be no more than a minor technical problem - certainly not enough of a problem to interrupt the general flow of discussion.

9   See, e.g. the wealth of detail in Sahlins, M. (1974), *Stone Age Economics,* London: Tavistock Publications.

7 The (re)distribution of wealth in anarchies

At the end of chapter 6 it was asserted that there is a need for a rough equality of wealth amongst anarchists if stability of an acephalous community is not to be undermined. Large differences in wealth tend to generate differences of interest. This can reach a stage where interests are not only different, they clash. Once that happens a basis for voluntary co-operation is weakened. An obvious possible solution to this problem has been put forward in the last chapter: fissioning. If there are inter-group clashes in the community then one group, say, should move to a tuath more agreeable to its interests. Socially that works quite well but does the fact that the present concern is economic make a difference? Fissioning could work in this case, too, e.g. if there is a very rich group and a very poor group, then one - quite possibly the latter - can simply move on. It could move on if there is a tuath sympathetic to it. But that is by no means assured. Say, for instance, an economic pattern has developed not in just one, or a few tuatha but generally. Further, this pattern contains the elements of capital economics to an extent approaching the peon relationship. In that case fissioning will not solve the problem presently confronting the poor. Within the limits of market control, the rich will be free to move at will; the poor, on the other hand, though free to move in an abstract sense, might be tied by circumstances to their lot - another aspect to the peon relationship. This material has already been given attention and there is nothing to be gained from rehearsing it. I take it that large differences in wealth *do* occasion divergent interests. Obviously divergence of interest can result in conflict - for instance when the poor man becomes beggar man, the beggar man might well steal from the rich man. So, how do we manage to keep whatever differences in wealth there are short of becoming a risk to the co-operative stability of a community?

Evidence from the historical *tuatha* is not helpful here. The present research has revealed nothing about how they managed to restrict what would otherwise be politically damaging differences in material wealth. That could be because the historical cases did not need to confront the problem, of course; it could have been that acquisition and possession of wealth were not important aspects of the lives of the ancient Irish. Alternatively it might have been but the evidence for how it was handled socially is lost. But whatever the reason for history's silence in this matter it obliges us to look elsewhere for means to voluntarily prevent wealth destabilising acephalous community. Do we begin, for example, by looking to the assembly for policy guidelines? And will that suggest that the assembly should deliberate on how much personal wealth is going to be allowed? If so how is this to be calculated? How is it to be controlled? What happens to the money "found in excess" of some people's allowances? Is collection of personal surplus and its redistribution to be detailed to an executive organisation? If so, is this not just another way for the state to re-emerge, i.e. through the genesis of one of its key functions, the exchequer? On the face of it, making the (re)distribution of wealth a matter for the assembly has considerable promise of making as much trouble as it solves. The highly personal nature of the issue (*my* money) catalyses the Nozick problem of favouring my case with strenuous but questionable enthusiasm. In what follows I shall discuss two other options that anarchists have put forward as means of limiting wealth differentials which, at the same time, are intended to avoid entanglement in the questions above and the danger of regressing to statist procedures. The first, communist anarchism,[1] though formally coherent and perhaps ethically exemplary will be rejected on strategic grounds. The second - which will be incorporated as an addition to the tuath system - will be called the moka.[2]

I begin with an outline of communist anarchism. History is segmented into epochs. The final epochal transformation will be from statist to non-statist society. The resultant "republic of ends" is a community whose members have an abiding commitment to a Kantian categorical imperative and will co-ordinate their public interests in the manner of a Rousseauian general will. The arrangement will not be flawless; human fallibility being what it is there is a chance of some normative backsliding (into egoism) so there will be a (small) need for coercive measures. But, by comparison with its rate of incidence amongst state-governed people, the amount of backsliding will be minute in post-statist (communist) society for the simple reason that such a society cannot be realised until people in general are profoundly and actively convinced of its worthwhileness. Communism will have been achieved when the state has withered away. Presumably, if this occurs then, whatever else society is, it *is* anarchic. Immediately prior to this the last, vestigial state will have been, of its own function, self-destructive. It has had two jobs: to socialise the means of production and the distribution of public goods. Once these have been accomplished there is nothing else for the socialist state to do ... except disappear. It might be a little difficult to imagine this process but that is no wonder, Levine says, if we consider the sheer magnitude of the event. We are in one historical epoch, an archic one, at the moment and how we picture possibilities is very much conditioned by that fact; our sense of the possible has at least some of its roots in experience and inheritance. Epochal changes are not just historical developments, processes which have an almost organic relatedness with their past. Epochal changes are *radical transformations*. Caught up in our epoch we cannot picture, in any concrete way, what the next will be like. Notwithstanding, we can (a) justify it as *the* normative objective for political endeavour and (b) get something like a formal fix on its essential configuration. For the moment I shall put to one side the issue as to why we should bring about this epochal change; it is not to the present point which is, we might remind ourselves, how can the distribution of wealth be regulated in anarchic society? Suffice to say that Levine (1987, pp.108-14) regards exploitation as an evil which it is imperative to eradicate. He believes the only way to eradicate it from the process of production is to over throw capitalism, which is achieved by destroying its protection by the state, and initiating the transitionary socialist state commissioned, as it were, to bring about communism.

Levine takes it that post-statist society must, to be post-statist, have three fundamental features to its composition. (The educational and socialising programs in all likelihood needed to persuade people, particularly erstwhile capitalists, of the greater value of communism and the collectivisation of the means of production must have been accomplished during the revolution and the consequential period of the socialist state.) These features are: *the general will, the republic of ends* and *material plenty*. Levine can be allowed to speak for himself as to what he understands by these. Firstly, the general will, a concept he (pp.162-3) takes from Rousseau:

> The transformation in human beings required for communism is, of course, psychological. [Coming to appreciate that preference structures are not fixed would be part of this process.] People must become more communal and more inclined to subordinate private to general interests. In Rousseau's ... sense, they must become more "virtuous" ... [T]hey must become more moral; more inclined to assess alternative courses of action as pure personalities adopting the standpoint of generality, not empirically distinct selves bent on improving their own positions.

Secondly, the republic of ends, a Kantian idea, is taken (p.168) to entail that:

> [Only those moral] maxims that are universal are warranted for moral agents. However, to will only what can be willed by any rational agent is, Kant argued, to treat the capacity for rational determination - in oneself and in others - as an end in itself. The categorical imperative is therefore equivalent ... to (absolute) respect for the autonomy of persons as bearers of rational wills. Thus rationality does not individuate: whatever is binding on one rational agent is binding on any other rational agent similarly circumstanced; and whatever is binding without qualification and regardless of circumstances is binding on all.

And the republic of ends is:

> an organisation of persons (conceived as bearers of rational wills) for making laws ... a 'legislature' that discovers the general will ... It is the end of the dictatorship of the proletariat. (pp.168-9)

And, thirdly, material abundance:

111

It is conceivable, though unlikely, that most of what we want could become absolutely scarce - rendering co-operation irrational. However, it is much more likely, ..., that barring exogenous interferences, means for satisfying human wants will increase. (p.157)

And:

Socialism and therefore communism depend on the massive development of productive forces. (p.159)

In sum:

The diminishing scarcity that makes socialism (...) materially possible and the transformations in human nature required for communism to be politically feasible make a moral solution to the Prisoners' Dilemma problem Hobbes and Rousseau identified tenable. (p.165)

In chapter 5 I said of Wolff's preconditions for anarchy that, were they to transpire, anarchy would follow almost trivially; there would be no need to argue about its validity and viability. Something similar can be said of Levine's conditions here. If people did, in fact, reason "from the standpoint of generality", following a psychological transformation; and if the weak deontological ("similarly circumstanced") and the strong deontological ("regardless of circumstances") aspects of the categorical imperative were adhered to; and if there were sufficient material supply "to make co-operation rational", then there would be no need to compel co-operation in the distribution of public goods. Using Hume's phrase, the problem of managing limited sympathies would have been dissolved. True, it would be logically possible for disparities in wealth to occur under these circumstances. However, this is unlikely to become politically septic. In the first place there is no obvious reason to amass personal wealth, no urgency to grab as grab can - the degree of gross material supply makes that silly. Secondly, the psychology of the community has altered; people no longer attach great value to *personal* distinction, in riches or other things. Thirdly, the categorical imperative creates a balanced reciprocity in all exchanges. Exchange becomes a co-operative enterprise designed to optimise utility disinterestedly. In short there is no longer a problem about PIs in a state of nature; there are no PIs.

This near-trivial achievement of its ends gives the scheme some argumentative appeal - not least for the reason that one of its objects is the present concern, namely the prevention of wealth differences becoming a political liability. The chances of it being feasible, on the other hand, are hampered by some practical impediments at the transition stage, at the point where any further moves depend on the success of the socialist government in discharging its commission. Consider:

1 Capital exploits labour,
2 Exploitation is an evil,
3 States protect capital exploitation,
4 To effectively combat the evil its protection must be destroyed.

---

5 Therefore, overthrow the capitalist state.

Stripped of all but the bare essentials this is Levine's point of departure on the road to anarchy. Exploitation is evil for two reasons, (1) it has unequal (unfair?) distributive effects and (2) these effects are "achieved through force" (p.111). I shall follow Levine without caveat on this point.

Let us say that in a capitalist economy the gross proceeds from production are parcelled out (roughly) into three budgets[3]: (a) servicing the means of production (the running costs of a farm, factory or whatever), (b) the cost of labour and (c) owners' profits, assuming there are any. The wage earners would be better off if what presently goes to (c) went to (b). Sometimes the per capita benefits from (b) and (c) are not that different; at other times they are very different - even extreme, as I illustrated with the peon relationship. Either way, without (c) - and (a) remaining unchanged - recipients of (b) are better off (so long as (c) funds are not then given to something completely different - charities, for instance). In general PI terms we can say that recipients of (b) will have an interest in (c) being redirected to (b) - worker control of the proceeds of production (means, too, most probably). It is not inevitable that worker management of the means of production requires the revolution prescribed in 1-5, above. But 1-5 is certainly a means towards

113

it. For the sake of argument, assume that we have, indeed, had a successful proletarian revolution the long-term aim of which is post-statist anarchy. In the meantime there is ground work to be done to bring about the necessary conditions for epochal change. This is to be managed by the socialist state. How will it manage? This is where the impediments begin to affect the plot.

One of the first things the revolution has brought about is the separation of the capitalist class from its property. If this dispossessed class is not simply to be killed off something else has to be done with it. Levine suggests that it, and anybody else whose enthusiasm for and understanding of the purposes of the revolution is less than unqualified, must be educated into seeing the justice of eradicating exploitation (shifting (c) to (b)) or forced into compliance. Indeed, it is vital that the revolutionaries succeed in divorcing the sometime capitalists from their predilection for living off their profits. A whole class, or even a portion thereof, surviving the revolution, resentful of its losses, threatens to jeopardise further revolutionary progress. I shall return to this first of the impediments presently, after having identified the second. Equally important to the progress of transition is that the revolutionary administration - Levine, in company with Marx, sometimes calls it the dictatorship of the proletariat - develops immunity to the counter-revolutionary temptations to be found in its way. These are not for material acquisition, Levine supposes, but their work does give them power to direct the lives of people in the community and the temptation is to retain that power long after it "should have been given back to the people"[4] - the very problem Rousseau foresaw with his magistrates come to haunt again. It is these two matters - the survival of a disaffected class and the possibility to develop another form of exploitation - which are the hurdles in the way of progress towards epochal change. It is not beyond question that they will arrest revolutionary progress. Nevertheless, their likelihood of doing so is considerable.

Something to be noticed about the unreformed capitalist class (call it C) is that what the revolutionaries (call them R) are trying to do to it must surely have considerable psychological effects on it, e.g. alienate its sympathies. Of course some members of C have been known to join R causes (historically, some R causes have been led by C-renegades) but, as a class, C can be expected to be hostile to having its property appropriated. Furthermore, it has means for tactical response to R initiatives. It can, and very often has, shifted its capital out of the revolutionary zone before R is sufficiently in control to prevent this. It can supplement this action by destroying immovable assets, i.e. scorched earth tactics. The result is that budget items (a), (b) and (c) are put beyond the reach of R ... and it might be without production plant, too. For Levine's plan the consequences of this are grave. His third vital condition to support the development of anarchy - material plenty - has gone. Perhaps the best R can do now is to collectivise labour and start, pretty well from the bottom up, to regenerate the means of production[5] - not enough to assure epochal transition. First strike action by C has created scarcity and, on Levine's understanding, scarcity strains the rational credibility of co-operation.[6]

There is another problem with C. Suppose that the revolution has got off to a more promising start and R has managed to seize a lot of C property. This property is then distributed to non-Cs on some sort of collective/non-private ownership basis. At the same time - if they are not simply to be "disappeared" - members of C are going to have to be assimilated into post-revolutionary society. Threatening C with penalties if it does not co-operate is short-sighted; it runs counter to the voluntary co-operation needed to achieve the revolution's objective. Yet, Cs are materially a great deal worse off after the revolution. On the face of it, they have no reasons to oblige R in any way at all, least of all by voluntary co-operation for they are PIs *manque*. Their preference orderings are fixed *outside* the ambit of universalist ethics in pursuit of a general will and, at the present, they have no interest in altering that. This has a spill-over effect: their animosity is not just something which affects them, it affects the whole revolutionary process: morally, politically and economically their hostile presence undermines progress. They can be described as a drag factor on the rate of progress towards epochal change. Is there anything educational the Rs can do which has a chance of altering Cs' values? The Rs could try an approach something like this: if you Cs co-operate with us we will *all* - including you - be better off than you were when your means of production exploited the proletariat; co-operation maximises returns. If you do not choose to co-operate our revolutionary policy permits us to force your compliance. This is, of course, a straight throffer and, in fact, not a bad approach to take with C. It is psychologically implausible to expect C in a body to about-face on its beliefs and values and morally mutate to pristine anarcho-communism without there being some manner of trade-off they can relate to. The throffer, on the other hand, appeals to values C

115

already has *and* establishes a bridgehead for its subsequent transfer to the Kantian normative position. And, of course, if C accepts this approach then its drag effect on progress towards epochal change will decrease.

As we might expect from a volatile situation like a revolution and the time immediately consequent, planning is liable to a great deal of uncertainty. Outcomes of strategies depend not only on the contingencies taken into account but on an indefinite number of others not anticipated. Even so we can put forward, tentatively, two strategy outcome predictions based on the above considerations.

(A) In the event of a contra-capitalist state revolution being either intended, or in its early stages, if C believes it will lose eventually, it increases its chances of surviving with its goods intact if it moves them out of the R zone. It can also weaken the immediate and intermediate efforts of R to control the means of production in the zone if it destroys the fixed production machinery. In this case R's project is up against a very substantial impediment: C has removed the finances for (a) and (b), ruined the means of R generating (a) and (b) and, in all possibility, C will have withdrawn its production know-how too. The work of revolutionaries has foundered on less. We can say of (A) that the drag effect of C has a very high chance of arresting revolutionary progress, perhaps by a factor up to 0.9.

(B) If R manages to seize the machinery of production before it is destroyed and enough of (a), (b) and (c) to keep production going, the chances are it will also have captured a goodly proportion of C (who lack the funds to escape). In this case, though the first phase of R action has been successful, C will still have a drag effect in stages 2 and beyond unless it is "won over" to the cause. A throffer, which connects C's preference orderings to R's, and, if effected, will make C better off post-revolution is calculated to motivate Cs to re-align their commitments from C to R. The drag effect of C might drop to 0.3, and diminish over time, all going according to plan.

If (B) is achieved, and other things being equal, we can say with a measure of confidence that Levine's revolutionary program will conduce to the emergence of an anarchy having within it self-balancing mechanisms that prevent wealth differentials upsetting community cohesion - self-distinction is no longer important.

But what of the caveat, "... other things being equal"? It turns out that quite a lot has to be equal to meet the requirements for communist anarchy. To make the point we will benefit from having two passages from Levine before us:

(1) In general, any psychological change that overwhelms the egoistic motivations that prompt defection can solve Prisoners' Dilemmas in principle. If players prefer to cooperate, cooperation, not defection, becomes the rational strategy. However, so long as private interest remains in force, the temptation to defect will persist. It can be countered but, in general, it cannot be overwhelmed. A political solution will therefore be unavoidable. To be sure, no association can hold together for long only through force. A disposition to cooperate, however inculcated or sustained, is indispensable. But failing the realisation of a general will, there is no substitute for states. In the final analysis, only the use of threat of force permits a sure and definitive escape from the state of nature. (p.164)

And:

(2) However, the moral solution, if universally adopted, would end the regime of private interest and therefore, in principle, the need for the state. If each player does only what would be rationally willed for all players, no one could adopt a strategy enjoining defection. For defection, by hypothesis, produces less than ideal outcomes; and no one could will that outcomes be worse than they otherwise might be. The point is not that in a Prisoners' Dilemma everyone wants everyone else to cooperate. That desire is eminently self-interested. The idea, instead, is that cooperation is enjoined for rational agents assessing alternatives impersonally. So long as deliberation proceeds from the standpoint of generality, cooperation will result. Insofar as Kant, following Rousseau, was right to insist that reason itself requires this standpoint, then *reason moves us from the state of nature to the republic of ends*. (p.164, italics added)

Reason, disinterested reason, is the driving force behind the successful transition from archy to communist anarchy (quotation (2)). Shorn of the fashionable language of game theory, Hobbes made the

117

same point: if the first party carries out its side it is rational for the second party to discharge its undertaking within an agreement. On the other hand, if negative reciprocity or free riding comes into play then coercion *must be* introduced to avoid this creating a degenerative state of nature (quotation (1)). Levine is not alone in reading the options as either co-operate or defect; he is in company with Nozick, Rothbard and many others besides.

This is worth thinking about, however. What if reason is not mono-directive? It seems to me that it is not and, if not, this seriously affects the chances of transition from state to anarchy if it be run on the communist program. Levine (pp.110-21) says there are three forms of exploitation: capital, organisational and skills. Capital has been discussed; the others only mentioned, so far. Organisational (sometimes called administrative) exploitation occurs through the vertical command structure of an organisation; in essence, the higher up (the party hierarchy, say), the greater the benefits to be had from exploiting the attendant power-giving opportunities. Differential rewards can also be distributed on the basis of the skills people have, i.e. if possession of certain skills is limited to comparatively few people but rather more need or want those skills exercised on their behalf it is again possible for the skills possessors to take advantage of the situation. Levine candidly acknowledges that organisational and skills exploitation are, of the three, the two most likely to survive into the socialist transition period. That could be so. For brevity in what follows, these exploitative groups will be called C for capitalist, O for organisational and S for skills. Now consider the socialist state, the transitional phase. It is agreed, by Levine anyway, that the socialist government will need administrators who, in turn, will need skilled advice, in order to carry on the distribution of public goods, albeit on a decreasing basis, whilst the psychological transformation throughout the community is being consolidated. In addition, of course, the need to build up material plenty could be helped greatly by recruiting the services of C. In that case O, S and C could find themselves in a structurally co-operative relationship.[7] To the extent that these groups are still infected with some degree of unregenerate private interests, why on earth should reason not suggest to them practical co-operation amongst themselves at the expense of those outside their group (the outsiders we call P)? This is limited co-operation; it is limited to an amalgam (SOC). The pay-off for SOC is much higher for it if it excludes P from its co-operative venture or at best distributes to P the bare minimum of benefits necessary to keep it biddable. In a superficially different guise SOC can become another manifestation of A+ Holdings. And, since this is a one-off game, SOC does not have to bother about the differences an iterated would game would make to its best long-term strategies.

The first thing to notice is the implausibility of supposing that reason moves us from the state of nature or state to the republic of ends. Reason, of a kind, *might* do so but, equally, reason of another kind might see the state (of SOC for SOC interests) rise phoenix-like from the ashes of the revolution.[8] Secondly, we notice that, normatively, the cause of R has been perverted because P, at least, has been sold short on its expectations. We might want to say that SOC has behaved unfairly; it has indeed, shamelessly letting down P which *depended* on O and S to raise its fortunes. Sadly there is cold comfort to be had from a Marxist point of view expressly because there is, from that perspective, no prior regard for fairness or justice. (This makes a Rawlsian view, that justice must determine any acceptable form of distribution of wealth and public goods, an attractive alternative to historical materialism.) Thirdly, the process of transition to communist anarchy has come to a halt. To get it going again is going to require another revolution it seems. But, of course, the pattern of events outlined above could easily recur; mayhap a cycle becomes endemic. Certainly there is no *reason*, in the limited sense used by Levine, why it should not. This empirical liability begins to present itself as a very substantial impediment to epochal change.

Perhaps it would be circumvented if the Kantian "moral solution" were "universally adopted". If that happened would it pave the way for epochal change becoming reality? What Levine expects from the categorical imperative is a radically transformed *de facto* standard of behaviour (including deliberation); a global normative disinterestedness which is god-like. Nothing less could "overwhelm", could eradicate the pathogen of egoism (1987, p.164). But here, as in the immediately preceding case, the disjunction is pure and exclusive to the point where it strains contingent credibility. Levine himself appears aware of this. In passage (1), above, he says of egoism that it can be "countered" but not "overwhelmed" and, "on the final analysis" statist force is the "sure and definitive escape from the state of nature". Perhaps revealingly passage (2) is not written in the indicative but in the subjunctive: if the moral solution *were* adopted this *would* propel us towards the republic of ends. The suggestion seems to be that we are probably stuck with (1) though

(2) is preferable. Further, it appears likely that, at least for the short and medium term, the best means that we can hope for in the regulation and distribution of public goods, on this account, is the socialist state (and always trusting that it does not fall prey to the unholy SOC alliance, of course).

It might be that Levine's communist anarchy is driven to these conclusions because it demands such an uncompromised moral regeneration. But does that imply that, short of such exacting deontological elevation, the pathway to anarchism is blocked? No. I shall now suggest a form of anarchic community which, firstly, accommodates the presence of self-interest. There are detectable traces of possessive individualism distributed so widely amongst humankind that if a political theory is to have temporal appeal this really must be taken into account. The challenge is: in order for communitarian anarchy to be plausibly attractive (in contrast to ideally attractive), people with some PI in them have to be able to imagine *themselves* in it. If it can accommodate some measure of PIism we are more inclined to give it credit for being feasible. Secondly, not only will there be allowances made for possessive individualism but, at the same time, wealth differences will be restricted so they do not threaten the cohesion of public interests within the community. Such is the moka system I advertised earlier. Thirdly, it will illustrate a major point essayed here: that anarchy is a potent alternative to archy when it has wide appeal including to those disinclined to alter their pre-existing preference orderings. Here it will be indicated that we do not have to choose the possessive individualist path or the Kantian one. The same acephalous social and economic order can lodge both.

When last discussed, the adapted tuath system replaced the state as distributor of public security through civil law and a social responsibility and liability network. With the addition of the moka it will now replace the state's regulative function over the economy.

Before showing how the moka works to stabilise communities, it should be clearly understood why these economically impelled "divergent interests" are a problem. What, after all, is so dangerous about divergent interests? That they can conflict? If so how? So far, all I have said is that if a poor man becomes beggar man he might very well become thief, at the rich man's expense. By drawing this out further we shall have prepared the way to seeing why, not only is the moka a very ancient custom in some acephalous societies, but is most sensible politically. One cause for anarchy becoming self-defeating is when it is saturated with negative reciprocity. The watch-word becomes: if something can be had for nothing, or at any rate for a good deal less than it is worth, so much the better. The worth of agents is gauged by the amount of acquisition they achieve. And a strong mix of emotions surrounds this phenomenon: greed, covetousness and envy. Ratiocination is channelled into cunning and deceit where plain old fashioned brutality seems in need of help. Result? "Warre of all against all", the *sine qua non* of self-defeating anarchy. In raw terms, if the acquisition of goods by individuals is the measure of success and there are "no holds barred" and long-term self-interest is overridden by the catalytic effect of highly charged emotional impulses, that is what we are left with by way of product of divergent interests. The spectre, as has been said often enough, is sufficient for many to legitimate the state, the only thing powerful and efficient enough to keep the lid on self-defeating anarchy.

It does not have to be supposed that *everybody* is hell-bent on profit from negative reciprocity. That would be a Stirneresque caricature. Closer to the generality of people is that they behave with a rather complicated mix of short- and long-term calculations, of general, balanced and negative reciprocity and an emotional scope which includes other-regarding feelings as well as selfish ones. Notwithstanding, there is enough of the content of the last paragraph around for it to be a serious threat to managing the distribution of public goods on the basis of voluntary co-operation.

Now to consider the place of moka in acephalous community. Economic wealth is a form of value which, as we have said, pre-disposes us to conflicting interests when very unevenly distributed. The moka system is a small-scale (by macro-economic terms), socially ritualised but voluntary form of exchange, combining aspects of general and balanced reciprocity, and resulting in a limitation to the extent of individual material acquisition. For our purposes the essential aspects of moka are:

1   Members of the community have private property in the form of land and other negotiable assets.
2   This they trade or retain as needs and wants require.
3   There are in the community more and less rich people.

4   But wealth is not gauged by the extent of material possession alone; in fact, a person with many possessions might be considered very poor.

5   And such a person will be treated with the pitying contempt we reserve for somebody who is poor through his own stupid fault.

6   People who, by dint of good trade, amass large stocks of negotiable assets have options: they can keep these (go for more even) and risk 5 or disperse them through the community.

Dispersal *is* a moka. This is usually done according to a rough schema. People in trade, unless something remarkable to a degree happens, seldom become rich through their own, unaided efforts. Usually somebody else did a small favour at least to help things along: inside information was given, negotiations were initiated through an intermediary, a line of credit extended, etc. The moka will settle such debts of gratitude. In addition, however, people who are apparently owed nothing will be made beneficiaries of it. If and when this happens it is important that gifts are handed out disinterestedly, at least to the extent that the giving does not cause jealousies between recipients and non- (or lesser) recipients.[9] People giving mokas are not expected to beggar themselves though they might reduce themselves to material subsistence. But there are more important consequences than that:

(i)   moka givers, though materially very much poorer after the event, are held in high regard by the community. What appears in one sense to be fairly general reciprocity on their part has a resulting balanced effect in terms of exchanged regard. Contrariwise, the materially covetous have reduced respect - in fact suffer negative reciprocity at the hands of the community; see 5, above.

(ii)   There is, too, a build-up in credit for moka-givers. The general beneficiaries of mokas are obliged to the donors. At some future time yet unknown, for a calling unknown, the recipients expect to give the donors something (in deed or kind). This is *not* contractual in any monetary sense. At the same time moka behaviour is very public; everybody in the community knows who got what and, consequently, who is obliged. Failure to honour obligations results in (5) again.

(iii) The balance of negative reciprocity, where, as here, exchange is public knowledge, weighs against free riders: trying to get something for nothing gets them very little for nobody will deal with them if they have tried it once. (If they try theft then the filid system, with the ultimate sanction of ostracism, comes into play.)

(iv) What satisfaction there is to be gained from the acquisition of material assets is allowed. But the moka process has a built-in control which prevents it creating divergent and, ultimately, conflicting interests. Assets are expected to be dispersed before that. Anyone inclined to be covetous has to consider: are the riches worth the social - and economic - isolation which will result? *Ad hominem* that is a massive price to pay.

(v) Moka giving is consistent with being an altruistic act and a self-seeking act. The motive is immaterial to the outcome and the outcome benefits both the individual in community and the community as a group. As a speculative aside to this: the moka could even be a means of enlarging the moral personae of PIs. They might come to see that what has value extends *beyond* material possession to intangibles - big-heartedness, greatness of spirit and what have you. If this occurred then, in a sense, the moka would partly overcome a practical impediment to Levine's program, namely his forbidding requirements for psychological transformation. It might be that habituation to the practice of moka will have transformational properties. The anthropological evidence indicates that the extent of this is not up to Levine's specifications but the sense of worth - of what it means to be a "big man" - amongst the highland communities of Papua New Guinea certainly extends beyond PIsm (but includes it).

At first glance it might be thought that the moka is all very well for pre-capitalist societies, but not for modern times when the measure of wealth is gauged by its conversion into a cash balance. But that is not quite so. To begin with, even in modern capitalist economies the measure of wealth is not exclusively a matter of doing a commodity-to-cash conversion sum. It still makes perfectly good sense for us to talk of other forms of wealth in our everyday speech: wealth of wisdom, charity, humour, etc. Still, it could be countered, these are pretty much downgraded nowadays: "He's got a wealth of knowledge but poor as a church mouse, I'm afraid". Yet wealth as measured in terms of non-material assets actually plays an important, perhaps even quite common, part in the world of capitalism. For a start, it is a bald fact that returns on dealings are optimised where the trading partners *trust* each other to keep their bargains. Quite apart from anything else this saves the cost of having to buy security against default. Not only is reciprocated trust dollar-wise, it has intangible pay-offs, such as the bonhomie or fellow-feeling shared by traders. In addition, think of the very appreciable number of rich - even not so rich - people who give money to philanthropic trusts or support endeavours in the arts and sciences. This behaviour is not unlike the moka. In one sense it is general reciprocity. However, there is a measure of balanced reciprocity, too. By their actions, donors gain standing, admiration, gratitude and whatever from recipients (artists, empirical researchers, etc.), indirect beneficiaries (patients whose conditions are cured by newly discovered procedures), and the community at large. It might or might not be counted on but the donors gain credit in the form of goodwill and, in turn, this credit can be called in: their business activities might be given special consideration, for instance, and that will increase profits. The *difference* between the philanthropy of business people and moka-givers is that, even when it is expected of the former (which it sometimes is) it does not contribute significantly to the evening out of wealth differentials.

So what is to be gained from playing out this idea of mokas? This: the idea is within the ambit of extant social psychology and experience. It does not require any massive transformation of nature. Indeed, it is close enough to something which is familiar to people whose activities are otherwise very far removed from tribal communities. And if it can actually limit dangerous wealth discrepancies then it advances the possible road to anarchy in having removed this large, practical impediment.

A negative *riposte* to that must surely come from possessive individualism. Of course there are different measures of wealth, the PIs can agree, but that does not alter the fact that each of us has a natural right to amass whatever wealth we wish and how we wish (so long as we do not infringe the like rights of others). There are neither prudential nor moral reasons why we must disperse our wealth in mokas. True, we do pay for services, such as security, but that is nothing like a moka ... nor should it be.

The objection has a certain vigour to it and is not lightly turned aside. My reply will be developed in terms of shifting our perception of costs and, by this means, giving PIs reasons to alter their preference perspectives. There was a time when the slogan (borrowed from Prudhon) "Property Is Theft" was the catch-cry of many romantic anarchists. Like most slogans it was hyperbole. On the other hand, that property *invites* theft is no hyperbole; it is indubitably true. From that we can develop an economic argument which, to the best of my knowledge, is not widely canvassed. Possessing large amounts of capital assets is itself expensive: its protection has to be paid for. This is one of the jobs of the state though quite often the state does not manage the job very well: successful property-related crime, including crimes of violence in the pursuit of property, exceeds the rate of successful police intervention. In which case state police are usually supplemented by insurance and, frequently, private police. The cost is now taxes plus insurance premiums plus payroll, without premiums and payroll being off-set by increased dividends; they only reduce losses (it is hoped). Also, the possession of great wealth increases the owners' personal risks. Perhaps in order to steal from them but for other motives besides, such as revenge (resulting from a shady deal) and envy (pure envy at the status or the desire to have it), the rich are at risk in their persons. So not only does their property need protection but they often have to - or think they have to - go to elaborate and costly lengths to guard themselves. The gross expenditure on protection does not stop there. There are administrative costs to the management of wealth - it has to be housed securely and so forth. There might be psychological costs as well: fear of being robbed and/or killed. My point is that, being not so rich as to have to create such an alien, not to mention risky, world for oneself is arguably better - great wealth differences create a Hobbesian state of nature between the haves and have-nots.

So money costs, one can almost hear the PI reply, but it pays too; besides, I *like* being rich. Two very common sources of pleasure in riches are the chances they provide for ostentation, for showing them off, and for extravagance.[10] These are psychological wants which wealth assists in the satisfaction of. The interesting thing then is that the moka can be used as a conduit to satisfy wants for both ostentation and extravagance. Indeed, as public displays go, few things can rival the moka for its ostentation and extravagance. Thus, psychologically it satisfies two very frequent motives people have to be rich. Furthermore, it has a prudential (perhaps even moral) pay-off which retention of wealth does not - quite the reverse, in fact. In the preceding paragraph the relationship of crime to PI wealth was mentioned. Aside from organised crime, which is, after all, the extra-legal aspect to capital, most theft is by the relatively poor of the relatively rich (rich man, poor man, beggar man, thief - again). The moka system, however, ameliorates this aspect to the human predicament. People are not that poor they have to steal. If they are moka recipients their needs, if any, are made up. And though being donors will leave them immediately and materially short yet, by having given the moka, they can call on all those who are now under an obligation to them. A major motive for theft is eradicated from the community. Even envy, as a motive for theft is undermined by the fact that, as Taylor puts it, there is a rough equality of wealth.[11] The flow-on effect of this is to subtract from the cost to the community as a whole the amount needed to secure its members from theft.

Another thing to notice about this approach is that it really does not matter if there is a measure of self-interested calculation going on. It does not matter in the sense that (a) the viability of the community is not threatened (destabilised) by it and (b) there is room for self-interest to prosper. True, material goods have to be "given" away sometimes but in return donors forge relationships which protect their future (legal) endeavours as well as community-wide trust and goodwill. Donors are well secured from mistreatment at the hands of other members of the community.

Now to sum up some implications which can be drawn from this chapter: firstly it is not questioned that epochal transitions could occur and, perhaps, have occurred. However, the Marxian-derived case that there will be an epochal transformation to anarchy is contingent on too many highly unstable variables which are located in a cluster at the transition state stage. Short of the pristine moral character of Aquinas' angels, any one of these variables, coming from S, O or C are immanently liable to arrest, even reverse, the process of transition.

The idea of tuatha, however, modified as the need has arisen, is a pathway to anarchy which has some hope of carrying the traffic, as it were, that an economy makes on an acephalous community. It is often claimed - as it is by Taylor and Levine - that developed capitalism, with its endemic tendencies towards hegemony, is a major stumbling block to the development of anarchy. Yet, ironically, the moka is, in fact, not a restriction on capitalism (being the usual prescription from anarchists) but an enrichment of it. It is an enrichment in the sense that the measure of wealth is replaced by *measures* of it, i.e. material goods can be exchanged for obligations now owed one and greatly enhanced esteem in the community. Thus there is more than one way of being instrumentally rich.[12] It turns out, on this account, that capitalism, as we know it, is a comparatively primitive form of wealth. Anachronistically we can make it a far more powerful economic system by going back to traditional acephalous community practices for advice.

Thirdly, whereas epochal transformation depends on a radical and general moral and psychological fillip, a tuath economy which has built into it the moka can accommodate a considerable measure of latitude along the egoist-altruist continuum. The moka is a throffer to egocentric PIs in the sense that though they are under threat of social disgust and some level of ostracism from the comforts of society if they are miserly, it also offers the reward of obligations due and elevated standing in the community if they are generous.

Fourthly, the moka raises the nett stock of publicly available utility without the need for such statist measures as taxation. In effect, the distribution of welfare goods is built into the economy rather than, as in very large state welfare bureaucracies, being a manifest burden upon it. To be sure I have not rehearsed the details of exactly how this could be managed (how does the moka provide medical treatment for the needy and poor? for example). However, in principle it is possible. The specifics of how to manage welfare through the moka system would require a substantial thesis on their own account though easy reference can be made to precedent in Marshall Sahlins' *Stone Age Economics*.

The modified tuath has political, legal and economic systems which have the prudential virtues of flexibility (they cope with a number of characters including the relatively intractable PIs), and resilience (the tuath can withstand quite a large measure of internal tension and, when that becomes too great, the community fissions rather than explodes into violence). At the same time, it must be owned, this pathway to anarchy could not manage the logistics of even comparatively small modern states, let alone those which measure their populations in hundreds of millions. That, though, brings the matter right back to the joke about not starting the journey here. It bears re-statement: this pathway to anarchy does not claim that acephalous communities can do the work of states just as well as states. States, as they have evolved, are quite possibly faced with challenges too great to be managed without considerable losses in personal freedom and responsibility. All that is claimed here is that the benefits of co-operative society, increased personal autonomy for example if one follows Wolff's line, might well be increased by taking a *different* way to the statist one. Indeed, this pathway is attractive to all those who would, after due reflection on their best possible worlds, rather do without states.

Notes

1 Following the Marxian derived work of Andrew Levine. See Levine, A. (1987), *The End of the State*, London: Verso. Note, moreover, this approach is not to be misidentified with Kropotkin's which, too, was called communist anarchism. See Kropotkin, P. (1909), 'Anarchism: its Philosophy & Ideals', *Freedom*, No.6.

2 As an acknowledgement to the peoples of Papua New Guinea whose word it is and amongst whom I first encountered the practice, though I understand similar events occur elsewhere. However, as with the tuatha, I shall depart from strict history or anthropology, as the case might be, where the need arises, e.g. to adapt the idea to the demands of topical circumstance.

3 There are others besides these, e.g. taxes, philanthropic bequests, etc., however, these have no bearing on the present point.

4 When this occurs, Levine calls it 'administrative and skills exploitation' by which, presumably, he means management manipulation and control abilities. See Levine (1987, pp.119-20).

5 The early economic history of the People's Republic of China is an instructive case-history on how this can be attempted. See Fairbank, J.K. (1988), *The Great Chinese Revolution, 1800-1985*, London: Picador, chapters 15-17.

6 I emphasise that this is Levine's view. It is correct within limits, e.g. if there is one indivisible good which can only be had exclusively, G., and which is desired by agents A and B then it is irrational for A and B to co-operate. However, it is uncommon for goods to be of this kind; mostly they can be partitioned. In this case co-operation under conditions of scarcity is *not* irrational. On the contrary, in PD terms, playing C,C still optimises returns.

7   Which might not be entirely harmonious. Marriage, for instance, is, formally, a co-operative relationship though, sadly, many marriages are far from so in practice.

8   For a more complete account of how and why SOC can channel a popular revolution to its own ends see Orwell, G. (1967), *Animal Farm*, Harmondsworth: Penguin.

9   Though some discretion is allowed, e.g. the moka giver discriminates in favour of a particular individual she wishes to be obliged to her.

10   These by no means come to the same thing: extravagance can be indulged in the utmost privacy; ostentation, by definition, cannot.

11   The psychology of miserliness falls outside the bounds of this discussion. Misers take pleasure in riches for their own sake; paying out, for any reason, counts as a loss. In the tuath misers can expect to be ridiculed and shamed. That will discourage those with a mild disposition in this direction. Hard cases will not be touched. Fortunately for the cohesion of the community, out-and-out misers are relatively uncommon.

12   Ignoring such transcendental forms of riches as those which might be stored up to our credit in Heaven.

8 Conclusion

The philosophical motive for this book was the apparent neglect, or if not neglect something very close to intellectual contempt, for anarchism in the "mainstream" of modern liberal political philosophy. At the outset it seemed to me worthwhile inquiring as to why anarchy seldom gets a look in on political philosophy, even as a sceptical gadfly. It has been noted that some people regard the question as to what justifies the state as otiose (at least now). So far as archists go, Nozick is all but singular in taking anarchy as a serious alternative to the state. The state is justified if and only if it is preferable to the best anarchic circumstance, he says. The present argument echoes Nozick's unfashionable challenge to contemporary political thought. The break with Nozick comes over the matter of what we can expect of anarchic society. To that I shall return in a moment.

Although it was emphasised at the outset that there is neither an assumption about nor argument for a general theory of human nature, yet the argument has focused on possessive individualists. To be sure they - possessive individualists - are common enough but that is not to the point. The point about PIs here is that they feature notably and consistently in accounts of why - like it or not - we need states. In modern political thought this line of reasoning goes back to Hobbes' justification for the state (reading him myopically for a moment) and comes right through to the present. Of course this idea is not a central feature in ideal socialist literature, for example, but then socialists are not PIs. In liberal thought, on the other hand, possessive individualists attract a considerable degree of attention and the state is justified here as often as not on what we might call the playpen defence: if they are allowed to range unchecked, PIs will inevitably harm themselves and each other; if, on the other hand, they are confined in a playpen then they can enjoy themselves there, securely protected from the damage wrought by unfettered freedom. To come back to Aquinas' remark, anarchy could only be good for angels. Possessive individualism has been set up here as the "hard case" for anarchy. Certainly within the line of thought which takes PIsm to be a core datum in political philosophy the presumption is that at least a conditional state is essential. Not all the cards are stacked against anarchy being taken seriously in this context but, it appears, the trumps are. My contention has been that the appearance is misleading, that anarchy is a viable political option for PIs; in some respects it suits them better than does archy. Of course their lives are still managed in anarchic society - they are still subject to legislation, legal responsibility, public opinion and social expectations - but management is acephalous. I have borrowed from John Dunn (1990) where he contrasts the "ideological fiction" (of intimate relations between government and governed) with the "massive social distance" that is the reality of modern states. What has been attempted in the preceding chapters is something of a reversal of this modern state. The ideological fiction becomes reality in anarchic community and social distance between rulers and ruled recedes to vanishing point.

To rehearse the development of the argument for the possibility of anarchism very briefly: Bramhall's attack on Hobbes' *Leviathan* led me to read the answer to the Foole in a new light. Hobbes actually allowed for the possibility of state of nature confederations but did not elaborate.

The question then was, what might happen with PIs in a state of nature? The question was tested against the Crusoe economics of libertarianism. It was found in chapter 2 that (a), by an invisible hand process, this opens the way to the peon relationship and (b) it is too spare a normative basis from which to settle a certain class of property dispute - and that cuts to the very roots of PIsm. At the very least, for PIs who have their long-term self-interest at heart, libertarianism is an imprudent pathway to take towards anarchy. Too much depends on circumstantial luck (e.g. being an A rather than a member of the B family). But even luck has a finite history; the peon relationship leads to tyranny or entropic anarchy just as much as insoluble property disputes lead to Nozick's feuding. But libertarianism has done yeoman service for the argument: it has shown us that viable anarchy needs more in the way of normative structure. How much more and of what kind are the next questions.

Nozick finds the major problem with anarchy (of an essentially libertarian form) is the threat it presents to security (of person and property) on account of over-enthusiastic personal natural rights claims which lead to feuding. By a succession of invisible hand moves PIs are led from the state of nature to the playpen, albeit the pen's structure is minimal. This is anarchy's darkest hour, so to speak, for it appears caught on the horns of a dilemma: on the one hand economic and political entropy and on the other, the state. At this juncture the tuatha system presents itself as an idea which, if put in place, forestalls Nozick's invisible hand because it functions as an inhibition on feuding *and* does not have built into it the motive force to develop into a DPA. Admittedly anarchy is still stalked by the possibility of the peon relationship - but that is managed in what follows.

If the state does not have to be invented, yet there are broad areas of concern which a pathway to anarchy must traverse if it is going to be prudent to follow it, viz., a political system, the provision of public security (against free riders) and means for preventing inequalities of wealth reaching a point where they destroy the community. These, respectively, formed the basis for discussion in chapters 5, 6 and 7 where the idea of the tuatha was adapted to meet demand.

In chapter 5 a legislative assembly was constructed on unanimous direct democratic lines so that the gap between rulers and ruled is closed. However, there is no pretension that what was created here will guarantee pristine unanimous direct democracy. Allowance has to be made for estrangement occurring from time to time. The fail-safe to cope with this is fissioning and, again, some time is given to showing how this is feasible. But at no stage is there a suggestion that political anarchy could manage the internal demands on and tensions within modern juggernaut states. But that is not an argument against anarchy having argumentative standing. It might even suggest there is something gravely out of sorts with such states.

To prevent as far as possible the negative reciprocity of free riding, the filid system of the tuatha was brought into chapter 6 and backed up by the addition of appropriate processes of socialisation. The lines of liability, for instance, work against the success of crime as a cost-efficient business concern. The problem for committing crimes of personal violence - if one can put it that way for a moment - is that evasion is so difficult. The lines of liability and the exploitation of modern means of public communication make this a very *open* society and that is inhospitable to the darkness and secrecy which seems to be the preferred environment of the violent. In addition, the practice of ostracism provides a powerful disincentive to free riding as well as being a very economic form of social hygiene. The same systems work against political crimes, e.g. attempting to usurp the acephalous form of the assembly. In a very general way the balance in crime management shifts from what punitive measures to impose on criminals to making crime itself an unattractive proposition.

Lastly, in chapter 7, I returned to the problem of wealth in so far as it is a problem when its inequalities of distribution create conflicts of interest. Anarchy could not survive that happening. Two possibilities for preventing it were mooted. The first, the Marxian argument, though formally coherent, was found to be of doubtful reliability. Those responsible for ensuring the process of transition to communism are too easily seduced into reproducing the state. The success of Levine's program is contingent on a purging of all vestiges of PIsm and its replacement with benign, generalised reciprocity. Short of that, the moka, if grafted with the tuath, not only prevents inequalities in the distribution of material wealth fracturing social cohesion but it also expands the idea of wealth in a way which, in comparison with capital wealth, makes the latter look for all the world a poor, crude thing. With the moka wealth ceases to be an instrument of negative reciprocity, allows the continued presence of PIsm and increases the stock of general utility.

Jordan (1986, p.1) has argued that the state is the primary source of all authority and controls all forms of autonomy; all other forms of authority and autonomy are derived. That may be a fact - as things stand now, for example. But it is not a necessary condition for a social, economic and political life free from immanent threat of entropic anarchy. Very far from it, practicable anarchy makes the state redundant. Of course it does not follow from that that practical anarchy has some generalised, imperative legitimacy. It is, however, a feasible alternative to the state in political philosophy, inasmuch as that it has standing. In addition, in comparison to the playpen state, it looks very like the more congenial option for possessive individualists.

133

Bibliography

Ackerman, B.A. (1980), *Social Justice in the Liberal State*, Newhaven: Yale University Press.

Addis, L. (1975), *The Logic of Society,* Minneapolis: University of Minnesota Press.

Allsopp, B. (1985), *Social Responsibility & the Responsible Society,* London: Routledge & Kegan Paul/Oriel Press.

Anderson, T.L. & Hill, J.P. (1979), 'An American Experiment in Anarcho-Capitalism: the Not so Wild, Wild West', *Journal of Libertarian Studies*, pp.9-29.

Aristotle (1969), *Nicomachean Ethics*, in Thomson, J.A.K. (trans), Harmondsworth: Penguin.

Aristotle (1957), *Politics*, Ross, W. (trans), London: Oxford University Press.

Bakunin, M. (1973), *On Anarchy*, in Dolgoff, S. (ed), London: Allen & Unwin.

Ball, T., Farr, J. & Hanson, R.L. (eds) (1989), *Political Innovation & Conceptual Change,* Cambridge: Cambridge University Press.

Barclay, H. (1982), *People Without Government: an Anthropology of Anarchism*, London: Kahn & Averill (with Cienfuegos Press).

Barry, B. (1965), *Political Argument,* London: Routledge & Kegan Paul.

Benn, S.I. (1975-6), 'Freedom, Autonomy & the Concept of a Person', *Proceedings of the Aristotelian Society*, Vol.76, pp.109-30.

Benn, S.I., et al. (eds) (1978), *Political Participation: a Discussion of Political Rationality*, Canberra: Australian National University Press.

Benn, S.I. & Peters, R.S. (1959), *Social Principles & the Democratic State*, London: Allen & Unwin.

Berlin, I. (1980), *Against the Current*, London: Hogarth Press.

Bowle, J. (1969), *Hobbes & his Critics*, London: Frank Cass.

Buchanan, J.M. (1965), 'Ethical Rules, Expected Values & Large Numbers', *Ethics*, Vol.76, pp.1-13.

Buchanan, J.M. (1986), *Liberty, Market & State*, Brighton: Wheatsheaf.

Buchanan, J.M. (1975), *The Limits of Liberty: Between Anarchy & Leviathan*, Chicago: Chicago University Press.

Burke, E. (1975), *Edmund Burke on Government, Politics & Society*, in Hill, B.W. (ed), London: Fontana.

Burnheim, J. (1985), *Is Democracy Possible?*, Cambridge: Polity Press.

Carter, A. (1978), 'Anarchism & Violence', in Pennock, J.R. & Chapman, J.W. (eds), ANARCHISM, *Nomos*, xix, pp.320-40.

Carter, A. (1971), *The Political Theory of Anarchism*, London: Routledge & Kegan Paul.

Close, D.H. & Bridge, C.R. (1985), *Revolution: a History of the Idea*, London: Croom Helm.

Cohen, G.A. (1979), 'Capitalism, Freedom & the Proletariat', in Ryan, A. (ed), *The Idea of Freedom*, Oxford: Oxford University Press, pp.9-25.

Cropsey, J. (1977), *Political Philosophy & the Issues of Politics*, Chicago: Chicago University Press.

D'Entrèves, A.P. (1967), *The Notion of the State*, Oxford: Clarendon Press.

Draper, H. (1978), *Private Police*, Harmondsworth: Penguin.

Dunn, J. (1990), *Interpreting Political Responsibility*, Cambridge: Polity Press.

Dunn, J. (1969), *The Political Thought of John Locke*, Cambridge: Cambridge University Press.

Dunn, J. (1985), *Rethinking Modern Political Theory*, Cambridge: Cambridge University Press.

Edwards, J.C.P. (1984), 'On the Role of Theism in Hobbes' Political Philosophy', University of Melbourne, unpublished M.A. thesis.

Edwards, P. (1985), 'The Human Predicament: a Context for Rights & Learning About Rights', *Educational Philosophy & Theory*, Vol.17, pp.38-45.

Fairbank, J.K. (1988), *The Great Chinese Revolution 1800-1985*, London: Picador.

Frey, R.G. (ed) (1985), *Utility & Rights*, Oxford: Blackwell.

Gellner, E. (1983), *Nations & Nationalism*, Oxford: Blackwell.

Giddens, A. (1986), *The Nation-State & Violence*, Cambridge: Polity Press.

Gierke, O. (1934), *Natural Law & the Theory of Society*, trans. Barker, E., Cambridge: Cambridge University Press.

Godwin, W. (1946), *Enquiry Concerning Political Justice*, in Priestley, F.E.L. (ed), 2 vols, Toronto: Toronto University Press.

Graham, G. (1986), *Politics in its Place*, Melbourne: Oxford University Press.

Gray, A. (1963), *The Socialist Tradition*, London: Longmans.

Green, D. (1986), *The New Right: the Counter Revolution in Political, Economic & Social Thought,* Brighton: Wheatsheaf.

Hampton, J. (1987), *Hobbes & the Social Contract Tradition,* Cambridge: Cambridge University Press.

Hayek, F.A. (1978), *New Studies in Philosophy, Politics, Economics & the History of Ideas,* London: Routledge & Kegan Paul.

Held, D. et al. (1983), *States & Societies*, Oxford: Blackwell.

Hobbes, T. (1969), *Behemoth*, Tönnies, F. (ed), London: Frank Cass.

Hobbes, T. (1968), *Leviathan*, Macpherson, C.B. (ed), Harmondsworth: Penguin.

Honderich, T. (ed) (1976), *Social Ends & Political Means*, London: Routledge & Kegan Paul.

de Jasey, A.E. (1985), *The State,* Oxford: Blackwell.

Jessop, B. (1987), *Studies in State Theory*, Cambridge: Polity Press.

Joll, J. (1980), *The Anarchists*, Cambridge (USA): Harvard University Press.

Jordan, B. (1986), *The State: Authority & Autonomy,* Oxford: Blackwell.

Kavka, G.S. (1986), *Hobbesian Moral & Political Theory*, Princeton: Princeton University Press.

Kavka, G.S. (1983), 'Hobbes's War of All Against All', *Ethics*, Vol.93, No.2, pp.291-310.

Krimerman, L.I. & Perry, L. (eds) (1966), *Patterns of Anarchy,* New York: Anchor.

Kropotkin, P. (1909), 'Anarchism: its Philosophy & Ideal', *Freedom*, No.6, London.

Laslett, P. (ed) (1970), *Philosophy, Politics & Society,* Oxford: Blackwell.

Laslett, P. & Runciman, W. (eds) (1969), *Philosophy, Politics & Society*, 2nd series, Oxford: Blackwell.

Laslett, P., Runciman, W. & Skinner, Q. (eds) (1972), *Philosophy, Politics & Society,* 4th series, Oxford: Blackwell.

Lee, R.B. & De Vore, I. (eds) (1968), *Man the Hunter*, Chicago: Aldine.

Lessnoff, M.H. (1978), 'Justice, Social Contract & Universal Prescriptivism', *Philosophical Quarterly,* Vol. 28, pp.67-73.

Lessnoff, M.H. (1974), *The Structure of the Social Sciences: a Philosophical Introduction*, London: Allen & Unwin.

Levine, A. (1987), *The End of the State*, London: Verso.

Locke, J. (1965), *Two Treatises of Government,* in Laslett, P. (ed), New York: Mentor Books.

Luce, R.D. & Raiffa, H. (1957), *Games & Decisions,* New York: John Wiley.

Mackie, J.L. (1979), *Ethics*, Harmondsworth: Penguin.

MacPherson, C.B. (1962), *The Political Theory of Possessive Individualism*, Oxford: Clarendon Press.

Melzer, A.M. (1990), *The Natural Goodness of Man: on the System of Rousseau's Thought*, Chicago: Chicago University Press.

Miller, D. (1984), *Anarchism*, London: Dent.

Monro, D.H. (1967), *Empiricism & Ethics,* Cambridge: Cambridge University Press.

Moore, B. (1979), *Injustice: the Social Basis of Obedience & Revolt*, White Plains, NY: M.E. Sharpe.

Murdoch, G.P. (1968), 'The Current Status of the World's Hunting & Gathering People', in Lee, R.B. & DeVore, I. (eds), *Man the Hunter,* Chicago: Aldine, pp.13-20.

Nozick, R. (1974), *Anarchy, State & Utopia*, Oxford: Blackwell.

O'Neill, O. (1986), *Faces of Hunger*, London: Allen & Unwin.

Orwell, G. (1967), *Animal Farm*, Harmondsworth: Penguin.

Paul, J. (ed) (1982), *Reading Nozick*, Oxford: Blackwell.

Paul, J. (1982), 'The Withering of Nozick's Minimal State', in Paul, J. (ed), *Reading Nozick,* Oxford: Blackwell, pp.68-76.

Peden, J.R. (1971), 'Stateless Societies: Ancient Ireland', *The Libertarian Forum*, April, pp.3-8.

Pendle, G. (1981), *A History of Latin America,* Harmondsworth: Penguin.

Pennock, J.R. & Chapman, J.W. (eds) (1978), ANARCHISM, *Nomos*, xix.

Perlin, T.M. (ed) (1979), *Contemporary Anarchism*, New Brunswick: Transaction Books.

Peters, R.S. (1967), *Hobbes*, Harmondsworth: Penguin.

Phillips, D.L. (1986), *Towards a Just Social Order*, Princeton: Princeton University Press.

Plamenatz, J. (1963), *Man & Society*, 2 vols, London: Longmans.

Popper, K. (1962), *The Open Society & its Enemies*, 2 vols, London: Routledge & Kegan Paul.

Popper, K. (1969), *The Poverty of Historicism*, London: Routledge & Kegan Paul.

Raphael, D.D. (1970), *Problems of Political Philosophy*, London: Pall Mall Press.

Rawls, J. (1971), *A Theory of Justice,* Oxford: Clarendon Press.

Rawls, J. (1972), 'The Justification of Civil Disobedience', in Beauchamp, T.L. (ed), *Ethics & Public Policy,* Englewood Cliffs: Prentice-Hall.

Riley, P. (1978), 'On the 'Kantian' Foundations of Robert Paul Wolff's Anarchism', in Pennock, J.R. & Chapman, J.W. (eds), ANARCHISM, *Nomos*, xix, pp.294-319.

Ritter, A. (1980), *Anarchism: a Theoretical Analysis*, Cambridge: Cambridge University Press.

Rothbard, M. (1982), *The Ethics of Liberty,* Atlantic Highlands: Humanities Press.

Rothbard, M. (1973), *For a New Liberty*, New York: MacMillan.

Rothbard, M. (1978), 'Society Without a State', in Pennock, J.R. & Chapman, J.W. (eds), ANARCHISM, *Nomos*, xix, pp.191-207.

Rousseau, J-J. (1990), *Emile,* trans. Foxley, B., London: Dent.

Rousseau, J-J. (1968), *The Social Contract*, trans. Cranston, M., Harmondsworth: Penguin.

Runciman, W.G. (1978), 'Processes, End-States & Social Justice', *Philosophical Quarterly*, January, pp.37-45.

Runciman, W.G. (ed) (1978), *Max Weber: Selections in Translation,* Cambridge: Cambridge University Press.

Ryan, A. (ed) (1979), *The Idea of Freedom: Essays in Honour of Isiah Berlin*, London: Oxford University Press.

Ryan, A. (1986), *Property & Political Theory*, Oxford: Blackwell.

Sahlins, M. (1974), *Stone Age Economics,* London: Tavistock Press.

Singh, C. (1985), *Law from Anarchy to Utopia*, Delhi: Oxford University Press.

Skinner, Q. (1978), *The Foundations of Modern Political Thought,* 2 vols, Cambridge: Cambridge University Press

Skocpol, T. (1979), *States and Social Revolutions*, Cambridge: Cambridge University Press.

Steiner, H. (1986), *An Essay on Rights*, Oxford: Blackwell.

Stirner, M. (1921), *The Ego and His Own,* trans. Byington, S.T., London: Jonathan Cape.

Stone, C.D. (1978), 'Some Reflections on Arbitrating Our Way to Anarchy', in Pennock, J.R. & Chapman, J.W. (eds), ANARCHISM, *Nomos,* xix, pp.208-14.

Strauss, L. (1953), *Natural Rights & History,* Chicago: University of Chicago Press.

Strauss, L. (1952), *The Political Philosophy of Hobbes,* Oxford: Oxford University Press.

Taylor, M. (1982), *Community, Anarchy & Liberty,* Cambridge: Cambridge University Press.

Taylor, M. (1987), *The Possibility of Cooperation,* Cambridge: Cambridge University Press.

Taylor, M. (ed) (1988), *Rationality & Revolution,* Cambridge: Cambridge University Press.

Taylor, M. (1988), 'Rationality & Revolutionary Collective Action', in Taylor, M. (ed), *Rationality & Revolution,* Cambridge: Cambridge University Press, pp.63-97.

Tilly, C. (ed) (1975), *The Formation of National States in Western Europe,* Princeton: Princeton University Press.

Tuck, R. (1979), *Natural Rights Theories: Their Origin & Development,* Cambridge: Cambridge University Press.

Tucker, B.R. (1893), *Instead of a Book,* New York: Haskell House Publications.

Tucker, D.B.F. (1985), *Law, Liberalism & Free Speech,* Totowa: Rowman & Allanheld.

Tucker, D.B.F. (1980), *Marx & Individualism,* Oxford: Blackwell.

Turnbull, C.M. (1961), *The Forest People,* London: Jonathan Cape.

Turnbull, C.M. (1973), *The Mountain People,* London: Jonathan Cape.

Wallerstein, M. & Przeworski, A. (1988), 'Workers' Welfare & the Socialization of Capital', in Taylor, M. (ed), *Rationality & Revolution,* Cambridge: Cambridge University Press, pp.179-205.

Ward, C. (1973), *Anarchy in Action,* London: Allen & Unwin.

Warnock, G.M. (1971), *The Object of Morality,* London: Methuen.

Warrender, H. (1957), *The Political Philosophy of Hobbes: His Theory of Obligation,* Oxford: Clarendon Press.

Wierck, D. (1978), 'Anarchist Justice', in Pennock, J.R. & Chapman, J.W. (eds), ANARCHISM, *Nomos,* xix, pp.215-36.

Williams, B. (1983), 'The Minimal State' in Paul, J. (ed.), *Reading Nozick*, Oxford: Blackwell, pp.27-36.

Winch, P. (1970), *The Idea of a Social Science*, London: Routledge & Kegan Paul.

Winston, G.C. & Teichgraeber, R.F. (eds) (1988), *The Boundaries of Economics,* Cambridge: Cambridge University Press.

Wolff, J. (1991), *Robert Nozick: Property, Justice & the Minimal State*, Cambridge: Polity Press.

Wolff, R.P. Moore, B. & Marcuse, H. (1985), *A Critique of Pure Tolerance*, Boston: Beacon Press.

Wolff, R.P. (1970), *In Defence of Anarchism,* New York: Harper & Row.

Wolff, R.P. (1968), *The Poverty of Liberalism*, Boston: Beacon Press.

Wolff, R.P. (ed) (1971), *The Rule of Law*, New York: Simon & Schuster.

Woodcock, G. (1983), *Anarchism,* Harmondsworth: Penguin.

Woodcock, G. (ed) (1986), *The Anarchist Reader*, Glasgow: Fontana.

Young, R. (1985), *Personal Autonomy: Beyond Negative & Positive Liberty*, London: Croom Helm.